urso Kae.

The Circle of Love

from Graham

Published by
The Bible Reading Fellowship
15 The Chambers, Vineyard
Abingdon OX14 3FE
United Kingdom
Tel: +44 (0)1865 319700
Email: enquiries@brf.org.uk
Website: www.brf.org.uk
BRF is a Registered Charity

ISBN 978 1 84101 750 1

First published 2010
Reprinted 2010, 2011
10 9 8 7 6 5 4 3 2
All rights reserved

Acknowledgments
Unless otherwise stated, scripture quotations are taken from the New Revised Standard
Version of the Bible, Anglicised Edition, copyright © 1989, 1995 by the Division of Christian
Education of the National Council of the Churches of Christ in the United States of America,
and are used by permission. All rights reserved.

Scripture quotations taken from the Holy Bible, New International Version, copyright © 1973,
1978, 1984 by International Bible Society, are used by permission of Hodder & Stoughton
Publishers, a member of the Hachette Livre UK Group. All rights reserved. 'NIV' is a registered
trademark of International Bible Society. UK trademark number 1448790.

Scripture quotations from The Revised Standard Version of the Bible, copyright © 1946, 1952,
1971 by the Division of Christian Education of the National Council of the Churches of Christ
in the United States of America, are used by permission. All rights reserved.

'Preparing the Icon' from Gillian Allnutt, *How the Bicycle Shone: New & Selected Poems* (Bloodaxe
Books, 2007). Used by kind permission of the publisher.

Extract from 'Lord of the Dance' by Sydney Carter, reproduced by permission of Stainer & Bell
Ltd, London, England, www.stainer.co.uk.

Extract from *Praying with Icons* (revised edition) by Jim Forest (Orbis Books, 2008).
Reproduced by permission of the publisher.

Excerpt from *Behold the Beauty of the Lord* by Henri J.M. Nouwen. Copyright © 1987, 2007 by
Ave Maria Press, PO Box 428, Notre Dame, Indiana 46556, www.avemariapress.com. Used
with permission of the publisher.

Extract from *The Christian Vision of God* by Alister McGrath (SPCK, 2008). Used by permission
of SPCK.

'And that will be heaven' by Evangeline Paterson, reprinted by permission of C. Rowland-Jones.

Prayer by Richard Harries, reprinted by permission of Richard Harries.

'Be still', 'Retreat' and 'Jeu d'esprit' by Ann Lewin, reprinted by permission of Ann Lewin.

A catalogue record for this book is available from the British Library

Printed in Great Britain by CPI Bookmarque, Croydon

The Circle of Love

Praying with Rublev's icon of the Trinity

Ann Persson

Acknowledgments

In writing this, my first book, there are some people that I would like to thank: John Laister, who first suggested that the material I used for a Quiet Day could form the basis of a book; Ann Lewin, poet, whose offer to read my manuscript and whose affirmation I valued highly; Joanna Tulloch, iconographer, who has been a great source of information and with whom I visited Russia; Naomi Starkey of BRF for her meticulous editing and for her encouragement; and particularly, my dear husband Paul, who uncomplainingly gave me the space to write and all the emotional support that I needed. It has been a journey together.

Contents

Chapter 1

The long look

The surgeon spoke: 'I will operate to repair the macular hole in your left eye.' That was good news but he went on to say that I would need to convalesce by lying face downwards for a fortnight with occasional short breaks. This, he explained, would enable the gas bubble injected into the back of my eye to stay in place and protect the surgery.

I was shocked. The idea of lying face downwards for such a long time was daunting. I am an active person and being still for a fortnight, let alone being face down, presented me with quite a challenge. However, with the help of my husband Paul and a friend, we made an extension to a wooden garden bed and cut a hole in it for my face. Padded well with pillows, it was actually quite comfortable, but I found it boring to have to stare at the carpet, so I asked for my favourite icon to be placed on the floor, where I could see it.

Andrei Rublev's icon of the Holy Trinity was my constant companion for the fortnight. I found myself drawn into the serenity and harmony of the three seated figures. The longer I gazed, the more engaged I became with the Father, Son and Holy Spirit and all that they represented. That is not surprising, because icons are intended to be windows on to the divine.

In a strange way, I felt a certain reluctance to pack away the bed and resume vertical living at the end of two weeks. I had been amazed by the kindness of friends who cooked meals for us and came to visit us, and I had delighted in the company of the icon, which had a very calming effect on me. What could have been a difficult experience had presented me with unexpected gifts.

I think it is true to say that whatever we look at for a long time has an impact upon us. I find that to be true when I visit an art gallery. The painting that I view the longest is the one I can recall best after I have left the gallery. I now prefer to be selective and spend more time in front of a few paintings than try to look at a greater number in a more superficial way.

Among my favourite books is Sister Wendy Beckett's *The Gaze of Love*.[1] In it she invites her readers to take their time to savour the paintings she has chosen, most of them contemporary, and to be led into discovery and on into prayer. To begin with, I find that I can't get anything much out of them, but then, as I practise patience and stay with the image, I start to see beyond the initial impression. With the aid of Sister Wendy's thoughts and my own, I am drawn into a deeper meaning, which leads to prayer.

Looking back

Very often, the pictures or photographs that surrounded us when we were children continue to have an influence on us. I remember being intrigued by a self-portrait of my great-great-great-grandfather that hung on the landing of my grandparents' home. Wherever I walked, his eyes would follow me. I would try to outrun him but those eyes were always watching me. Our children and grandchildren have been equally fascinated by him as he has now taken up residence in our home.

When I was eight, I was sent away to a boarding school in the Yorkshire Dales. It was a very unhappy experience: I felt trapped and isolated, far from home and from those I loved. I vividly remember a picture that hung in my classroom. It was in black and white, a print taken from an engraving, and it depicted Jesus as a shepherd climbing down a rock face to rescue a sheep perched precariously on a ledge. The sheep was caught in brambles and looked very pathetic. The shepherd was reaching out, one hand holding on to his staff for balance and the other gently outstretched towards the sheep. Day after day I would look at that scene, and even today I can still see it clearly in my mind's eye. It made a great impression on me. As a child, I may not have understood why it resonated so strongly with me, but, in retrospect, I imagine that I was subconsciously identifying myself with that lost sheep. I, too, wanted to be found and rescued.

As a student in London, I developed a personal faith in Jesus Christ. The picture I remember from that period is Holman Hunt's *The Light of the World*. The artist has painted the figure of Jesus standing outside a closed door. The figure wears a simple crown on his head, denoting kingship, but it is entwined with a circlet of thorns. He is dressed in a plain white robe with a richly embroidered cloak over his shoulders. He carries a lantern in his hand that sheds light on his face and also on the weeds growing outside the door, which gives the impression of having remained closed for a very long time. He patiently knocks, hoping to be welcomed in—for there is no handle on the outside of the door, only a knocker. This painting was brought to my attention by a friend, who patiently listened to my questioning and was able to direct me towards Jesus, the Saviour and Light of the World. I made a commitment of faith, responding to his knock and opening the door of my life to him. I kept a copy of the painting in my room as a reminder of the transaction that had taken place. I had been found and rescued.

In the later years of my life, Rublev's icon has come to mean a great deal to me. It invites me to be with the Trinity— at home with them. It reminds me of some words that Jesus spoke to his disciples on the eve of his death. He said, 'Those who love me will keep my word, and my Father will love them, and we will come to them and make our home with them' (John 14:23). The scene has a sense of home about it as the three figures sit around the table.

I have become fascinated by the icon of the Holy Trinity. It has led me on a journey of discovery not only about the icon itself but also about iconography in general (of which I was very ignorant), and on into what it means to be caught up in the life of the Trinity. This book is an attempt to share that journey with you; no doubt you will make your own discoveries along the way.

At the end of each chapter, I will provide some suggestions for further thought that you can use if you choose to do so.

⁓ For reflection ⁓

Whatever we gaze at for a long time, we remember.

Can you think of a painting, a photograph, a quotation or an image that has been important to you, maybe as a child or in later years?

What impression does/did it make on you and why do you think that is so?

Note

If you would like to have your own print of the icon, you could find one on the internet or in a book, or you could buy one from a Christian bookshop.

Chapter 2

About icons

Like a box of Liquorice Allsorts, we human beings come in a range of colours, shapes and types. Some of us are cerebral people, who live mainly through the intellect and relate to concepts and analysis, while some are emotional and live quite a lot by feelings; yet others are highly aware of their senses and respond to creation, colour and the visual. Then there are those who live predominantly by their intuition, not knowing quite how they form their opinions but proving uncannily accurate in their hunches. Some of us are extraverts, finding energy in being with other people, and others are more introverted, with a rich interior life. The extraverts need to speak in order to think, but the introverts need to think in order to speak. We are, of course, a mixture of all these types to a greater or lesser degree. It is just that we have preferences in the way that we relate to the world and its people.

It was not until I was in my 50s that I began to be aware of who I really am. Having had a poor education (although it was paid for), I had spent years feeling academically inferior, unable to be articulate or take part in debate because I did not have the confidence to express my opinions. As a result, I became a listener—which has, incidentally, stood me in good stead ever since. When the children left home, there was that awkward space in my life—I believe it is called the 'empty nest syndrome'—and I was not sure who I was or what my role in life would be in future years. I enlisted for a counsellor training course, in which, quite apart from learning how to be alongside others, I began to discover and, for the first time, value the intuitive side of my character. It was like a key turning in a lock. A door opened, that I could pass through to live in greater freedom. I didn't have to be what I thought I should be. I just had to be me. I could trust my judgments and run with my imagination. I began to identify what energises me. I could say 'yes' to being excited by music, colour, movement, art and the natural world around me.

This discovery has also been a help in my spiritual life because, in approaching God, those same 'yes' factors have come into play. I now find that I am eased into his presence by music, art, movement and his amazing creation. So it is not surprising that I intuitively responded to Rublev's icon, without knowing much about it.

Over the centuries, people have wanted to convey spiritual realities through visual images. Churches, museums, galleries and homes throughout the world display religious works of art. Paintings abound depicting the annunciation, Christ's nativity and baptism, his transfiguration, crucifixion and resurrection, Mary the mother of God, the apostles and the saints.

Art in the early Church

Portrait painting was popular in the Roman Empire at the time of Christ and there is a belief that an image of Christ himself dated from his own lifetime. Early in the fourth century, Eusebius wrote in his *History of the Church*, 'I have seen a great many portraits of the Saviour, and of Peter and Paul, which have been preserved up to our time.'[1] I wonder what they would have looked like—olive-skinned or fair, bearded or clean-shaven, strongly built or slight, dark or flaxen hair. We can only speculate.

Recently my husband and I visited Rome, and we were taken to see some of the catacombs. I say 'some' because there are many miles of catacombs around Rome. They are underground labyrinths made up of burial chambers tunnelled out of the soft, volcanic tufa rock. Some were Jewish burial sites, some were pagan, but most were Christian. In the first three centuries, Christianity was illegal in the Roman Empire and Christians were often brutally persecuted because of their faith. They needed secret places to bury their dead—hence the tunnelling of the catacombs.

Often, when persecution was at its fiercest, Christians would hide in the honeycombed cemeteries beneath the ground, in fear for their lives. They scratched symbols of their faith on the walls, and fragments of their frescoes remain to this day. We could make out three men praising God in the fiery furnace, Noah in the ark, the eucharistic meal, Jesus raising Lazarus from the dead and Jesus as the good shepherd, carrying a lamb on his shoulders. There were symbols of a fish, a dove and an anchor. In the absence of the written word, these simple drawings became powerful reminders of the God who could meet them in their own suffering, and of Jesus who said, 'I am the resurrection and the life. Those who believe in me, even though they die, will live, and everyone who lives and believes in me will never die' (John 11:25–26). They looked upon the catacombs as resting places, where their dead relatives and friends, many of them martyrs, would await the resurrection.

We were impressed by the fact that it was not enough for those first Christians to write inscriptions; they wanted to have visual images as well. I suppose this is not surprising, for all around us is a wonderfully visual world, created by God for us to inhabit. We are made in his image and so creativity is part of our nature, too. We express it through art, words, movement and music. It touches the soul, and, when we want to convey feelings, thoughts and worship sparked by a sense of the divine, we use these various expressions. So John wrote his Gospel; Handel composed the sublime 'Hallelujah' chorus in his *Messiah*, Michelangelo sculpted the *Pieta* and Rublev painted his icon of the Holy Trinity.

With its use of icons, the Eastern Orthodox Church has particularly focused on the visual. An icon is not the same as a picture. The word 'icon' comes straight from the Greek *ikon*, which means 'image'. It can be applied to a mosaic, a fresco, a statue or paintings on wood that represent a historical event in scripture or the life of a saint. It is an ancient art and a sacred art. Icons are not intended for decoration or as instruction for the uneducated (as stained-glass windows were in Western churches). They are a gateway to the divine and, as such, they are aids to worship.

Purists would speak of icons as being 'written', not painted, because iconography is not simply a form of art. Rather, to write an icon is to make the word of God present, and it is important that worshippers should learn to 'read' them. However, for the purposes of this book, I shall use the word 'paint', which describes the technique of creating an icon.

The destruction and revival of iconography

In the eighth and ninth centuries, at the time when Islam was rapidly spreading into areas that had formerly been Christian, there were arguments over icons. Emperor Leo III of Byzantium saw the practice of venerating icons as idolatry. He quoted the commandment, 'Thou shalt make no graven image nor any likeness of any divine thing' (Exodus 20:4). The result was that from around AD726 until 842, there was such a great destruction of icons and religious images (described as 'iconoclasm') that, sadly, little remains from the period before 726. The remote monastery of St Catherine at the foot of Mount Sinai was built in the sixth century, reputedly on the site where Moses saw the burning bush (Exodus 3:2). By the end of the seventh century it was no longer part of the territory of the Byzantine Empire, so the monastery's icons escaped damage during the period of iconoclasm. Consequently, it houses the best collection of early icons, among which is the sixth-century Christ Pantocrator or 'The blessing Christ'.

There was a respite from the iconoclasm between AD787 and 815. The second Council of Nicea was held in 787 and strict guidelines were laid down for the use of icons. A distinction was drawn between the Greek words for 'worship' (*latria*) and 'veneration' (*proskynesis*). Worship belonged to God alone, so icons were not to be worshipped but venerated. Their purpose was to be 'a window opening on to the divine' or 'a door to Paradise'; they would be held in deep respect, honoured for their qualities of holiness and used as aids to worship.

The Council also ruled on the subjects that could be painted in icons. Only God the Son could be directly represented as he became incarnate and was made man. There was to be no direct representation of God the Father or God the Holy Spirit.

One of the most unfortunate chapters in the history of the Church took place around 1054, when the 'Great Schism' occurred. It resulted in a break between the churches of the Catholic west and the Orthodox east, to each church's detriment. There were political factors that led to the split—rivalry between Latin-speaking Rome and Greek-speaking Constantinople, and a disagreement over the authority and supremacy of the Pope. But there was also a doctrinal factor—the controversy over the 'filioque' clause in the Nicene creed. Whereas the Eastern church believed in the Holy Spirit as 'proceeding from the Father'; the Western church altered the phrase to say that the Holy Spirit proceeds 'from the Father and the Son' (*filioque* means 'and from the Son'). This has remained a major theological point of difference between the Catholic and Orthodox churches, although more latterly there have been tentative moves towards reconciliation.

Russia converted to Orthodox Christianity in 988, under the influence of Greeks from Byzantium, who brought their icons with them. For the first 200 years or so, Russian icons were dominated by the Greek style, which can appear severe and rigid in composition. When the Mongol invasion in the 13th century cut Russia off from Byzantium, however, the Russian artists gradually developed their own distinctive style of iconography, which is generally more fluid and curvaceous than the design of icons from elsewhere. Their icons are typified by qualities of tenderness, harmony, peace and the warmth of the Holy Spirit.

The golden age of Russian iconography was in the 14th and 15th centuries, partly due to the rise in monasticism. One of the greatest icon painters of that time was Andrei Rublev. His works can be seen in the Cathedral of the Annunciation in Moscow and in the Dormition Cathedral in Vladimir, but the icon of the Holy Trinity, for which he is most famous, now hangs in the Tretyakov Gallery in Moscow. He painted at a time when Russia was in a state of chaos. There was much civil unrest and division among the people, as well as brutal attacks from the Tatars, fierce nomadic tribes from Mongolia. Russia found itself under Mongol occupation from about 1230 to the middle of the 15th century. For over 300 years, the period of the Renaissance in the West, it was cut off from European culture and inevitably became inward-looking.

The art of iconography continued to flourish in Russia until the reign of Tsar Peter the Great (1672–1725), who favoured imitation of all things Western, whether in architecture, fashion or art. His successors continued with the same attitude, so that, by the middle of the 18th century, there were very few who painted icons in the traditional way.

1917 brought the Bolshevik Revolution and, with it, further persecution of Christians. Once again, icons were destroyed, or sold to foreign markets. Icon painting was prohibited in the Soviet period so painters were forced to work in secret. At the end of the 1980s, however, the prohibition was lifted. Large numbers of icon painting studios have opened and are working in a variety of styles for both the local and the international market. There has been a renaissance in classic iconography, largely due to the uncovering and restoration of many ancient icons. Interest has spread beyond the Orthodox Churches and people from different churches across the world now value icons as a way into silence and prayer. Many a Russian home has icons hanging on the wall in the *krasny ugol*—the 'red' or 'beautiful' corner.

Preparation for icon painting

When iconographers decide on the subject that they want to paint, they do not try to be original. Instead, they will find ancient icons depicting the same subject and follow tradition in their style and composition, though they will not copy slavishly the works of others. Leonid Ouspensky writes, in his book *The Meaning of Icons*:

Tradition never shackles the creative powers of the iconographer, whose individuality expresses itself in the composition as well as in the colour and line. But the personal here is much more subtle than in the other arts and so often escapes superficial observation... Although icons are sometimes remarkably alike, we never find two absolutely identical icons. Icons are not copied but painted from.[2]

Therein lies the difference. An iconographer does not set out to reproduce a biblical scene or the image of a saint using dramatic gesture or movement. The faces of those represented rarely express emotions. The icon is silent; there are no open mouths. Rather, the faces suggest qualities such as compassion, love, purity, humility and patience in suffering. The physical pain that Christ must have suffered as he hung on the cross is not shown. Instead, we become aware of his dignity, his sacrificial love and his free offering of himself for the sins of the world.

In Western art, we are used to seeing paintings that make use of perspective, where the lines of a composition lead to a vanishing point. In icon painting, the vanishing point would seem to be the viewer. Use is made of reverse perspective so that the image comes to meet us, engage us and draw us in. It is almost as if we don't look at the subject of the icon; instead, the image looks at us.

The space and silence of an icon invite contemplative prayer. This is a space that, strangely, is not empty and a silence that is not 'dead air'. It allows for the presence of God and the warm heartbeat of the divine, if we allow ourselves to be still and open before it.

The icon is born out of silence, prayer and devotion, for an iconographer needs to be a person of faith—one who leads a disciplined moral life, not seeking personal glory but the glorification of his or her subject. For this reason the finished icon is not signed and, usually, little is known of the iconographer's identity. This is true in the case of Andrei Rublev. Hardly anything is known about him as a person, only as a painter. Very often, iconographers are monks, as the monastic lifestyle—with its emphasis on stability, poverty, chastity and obedience, linked with love and humility—is conducive to painting spiritual subjects. Also, through his attendance at the church's daily pattern of services, a monk would be familiar with the yearly cycle of festivals and saints' days in the liturgical calendar. Creating an icon is not just about mastering the skills of a craft; it is also about prayer, fasting and meditation. It is to be seen as heavenly work given by God, and a time of disciplined preparation of heart, mind and soul is of the utmost importance.

This idea is captured in a poem by Gillian Allnutt, in which she imagines Andrei Rublev instructing his apprentices in painting an icon of John the Baptist.

Do not imagine, now, the austere sad face of John.
Before the snow falls, go to the forest.
Bring wood for the board. For days, while the stove remains
unlit in the studio, work the wood with chisel and plane
until it is smooth.
Break the ice on the water-butt then.
Prepare and apply to the board the first thin layer of gypsum
like a skin. Stretch the canvas. Then put on
a second layer of gypsum. When it is hard and dry, like bone,
rub it down until your shoulders are tired.
Draw the outline of John from the book of tracings,
the Authorized Version.
Begin your illumination with the background. Green.
Bring a bowl of eggs from the monastery farm.
Let him come loud and clear as a locust in your listening
to his God, ours. Break the eggs.
Use only the yolk for the dilution of your colours.
In the silence of falling snow and the imagination's
cold dark halls, you'll know your own
austerity and John's. [3]

In Jim Forest's book, *Praying with Icons*, he records a typical prayer of an iconographer before he begins his work:

O heavenly Master, fervent architect of all creation,
light the gaze of your servant,
guard his heart and guide his hand,
so that worthily and with perfection
he may represent your image,
for the glory and beauty of your Holy Church.
In the name of the Father, Son and Holy Spirit,
now and forever and unto ages of ages. Amen. [4]

This iconographer would then make the sign of the cross, examine his conscience, ask forgiveness for his shortcomings and pardon any who have wronged him. Only then is he ready to begin.

The technique of iconography

I was discovering a little more about icons—probably only as much as the tip of a big iceberg—but I wanted to know about the techniques for painting them. Here I was helped by Joanna Tulloch, who, with a group of friends, meets for icon painting on a monthly basis. She invited me along to be an observer.

Joanna told me that, in icon painting, earthly materials are used to depict a heavenly subject. The vegetable world offers wood for the panel; oil, amber or other resins for the varnish; and flax for the linen covering. From the animal world comes egg, which is used to bind the pigments; the sable or squirrel hair for the brushes; and size (glue), often made from rabbit skin. The mineral world provides the colour pigments, the gold leaf and the ground alabaster, marble or chalk whiting for the *gesso* (plaster). The remaining ingredient is water.

It seems that most icons are painted in egg tempera on dry, well-seasoned, non-resinous wood such as lime, birch, alder or cypress. The panel chosen for the icon must be free from knots. Preparing the surface of the wood can take up to a week. First it is planed, then routed to create a recess for the painting and, by implication, a frame around it. This allows the hand to rest on the frame and avoid touching the paint while it is being applied. Two horizontal wooden struts of hard wood are inserted into the back of the panel to prevent warping and cracking. The surface of the panel is finely scored and covered with a liquid size, which is obtained by dissolving the rabbit skin glue in hot water. The panel is then left to dry.

The next step is to glue on a piece of loosely-woven linen. There are two reasons for doing this: it prevents the wood from cracking and it binds the plaster, or *gesso*, to the wood. This is followed by the complex procedure of applying the *gesso*.

To prepare the *gesso*, alabaster, marble or the highest-grade chalk is ground into fine powder, mixed with glue and applied to the linen, keeping the coating as thin as possible. Care has to be taken that there are no air bubbles or other imperfections. There can be between eight and 20 layers of *gesso*. Each application is allowed to dry and is then thoroughly cleaned and smoothed so that there is no surplus of chalk or dust left behind.

When the desired number of layers is complete, the panel is finished off with fine sandpaper or rubbed over with a smooth, flat stone to produce a polished, silky texture. At last it is ready to have the design transferred on to the plaster panel. One way is to lay a paper pattern over the panel and prick along the main outlines using a sharp tool, such as a stylus. The outlines are then scored by joining up the dots so that the surface is indented.

The colours used in iconography are mineral pigments and natural organic colours. I watched Joanna make up the egg tempera. She lightly chipped away at the top of an egg to make a sizeable hole and tipped the contents into her hand, passing them from hand to hand until the egg white had slipped away. The yolk was then gently washed, as was the inside of the shell. She pierced the sac and let the yolk run back into the shell. A few drops of vinegar were added and the shell was filled up with water. The ingredients were mixed gently but thoroughly before being decanted into a container. The mixture, I was told, would keep for up to ten days in a fridge.

Next, her chosen pigment was ground into an even finer powder on a glass panel, using a glass pestle. A little of the egg mixture was added until it was the right consistency for painting. The paint dries as quickly as watercolour but is not so easily washed off. Its durability and resistance to fading make it a very suitable medium for icon painting.

Iconographers are free to a certain extent to choose their colour combinations and tones, but they are bound to paint the garments worn by the figures in symbolic colours. Blue is linked to divinity and to heaven; green is for youth, freshness, fertility and plant life; red, the colour of blood, stands for life, vitality and beauty; orange-red is used for fire, fervour and spiritual purification; brown is the colour of earth and poverty; purple is associated with splendour, riches and power; white expresses purity, innocence and radiance; gold is associated with sanctity, glory and the divine life of God.

If some areas are to be gilded, such as the background or haloes, this is done before painting on the colours; otherwise the gold would stick to the paints. Applying gold leaf is a skilled and delicate process. First, a special mud-like preparation called *bole*, made from red or yellow ochre, is applied to the icon. The gold leaf is carefully laid over it and burnished with a smooth agate stone.

The colour is painted on in layers, beginning with the darkest and ending with the lightest. Layer upon layer is built up, with the brushes becoming ever finer, and bit by bit the image forms. The process is long and concentrated.

Sometimes translucent layers are applied to give a sense of inner luminescence. Finally, the outlines may be redrawn and bright touches added, using white or liquid gold. The folds of a garment or its embellishments are highlighted for effect.

The name of the icon's subject is inscribed on it for identity and the completed icon is left to dry for a few weeks. It is then covered with a glaze of *olipha* (boiled linseed oil), to which is added amber or other resins. The varnish protects the icon from damp and light, but it also has an effect on the colour, bringing out the rich, warm hues and adding depth and further translucence to the image.

There is a very important last step, once the icon is dry. It is placed on a church altar and the iconographer is the first to pray before the icon, thanking God for the grace given to paint the holy image. The priest and others bless the icon with their prayers and only then can it be given to the church, monastery or home for which it was commissioned.

Learning all this, I became aware of the dedication of the iconographer, firstly to God and then to the image that he or she is depicting. It is indeed a spiritual work that they undertake and they do so with reverence. They will continue in prayer as they work, asking God for his guidance at all points, and they will keep silence. They will work as if they are working in front of God himself and it will be for God's glory, not their own. The icon is born of silence, humility and prayer, and this is manifest in the resulting piece of work. In turn, it leads others into silent worship.

As my respect for the work of iconography grew, an idea took root in my mind and a longing was born in my heart— to travel to Moscow to see Rublev's Trinity icon for myself.

To my amazement, Joanna came up with the same idea and suggested a visit to the Tretyakov Gallery. I readily agreed to her suggestion, although it meant braving a Russian winter.

~ For reflection ~

I am impressed by the patience displayed in the preparation for painting an icon. Nothing is hurried. Every stage, from smoothing the surface of the wood panel to varnishing the completed icon, is given its own unhurried time. This is a challenge to my praying. In the busyness of life, I find that it is all too easy to rush into my place of prayer and then rush out again.

I ask you, as I ask myself, whether it is possible to set aside an extended time for prayer and meditation. How will we prepare ourselves for it, both in an outward practical way and in the orientation of our hearts and minds?

Can we allow ourselves simply to 'be' with God?

Be still

You do not have to look for anything,
Just look.
You do not have to listen for
Specific sounds,
Just listen.
You do not have to accomplish anything,
Just be.

And in that looking
And the listening
And the being,
Find
Me.
ANN LEWIN[5]

Chapter 3

To Russia

It was bitterly cold and snow was falling as we made our way to the Tretyakov Gallery in the centre of Moscow. It is named after Pavel Tretyakov (1832–98), a wealthy Moscow merchant and industrialist who acquired works by Russian artists of his day. His aim was to create a collection that would one day grow into a museum of national art, and in 1892 he proudly presented his already-famous collection to the Russian nation. Since then, the collection has grown considerably and now houses not only 20th-century paintings, drawings and sculptures but also a collection of Russian icons of the 15th to 19th centuries. In the church adjoining the building, one of Russia's most celebrated icons, the beautiful twelfth-century icon of The Virgin of Vladimir, is on view.

As we stepped inside the building, the heat wrapped itself around us in welcome. We put on the plastic overshoes that were provided and padded down the corridors to the place where Joanna knew that the Rublev icon was displayed. I felt excited at the thought of seeing it. As we turned each corner, I had a growing sense of anticipation and then, suddenly, there it was, unmistakable in its cool, calm beckoning. I was not prepared for its size. It measures 55 inches in height by 44 inches in width and is safely protected in a glass case.

It was the end of the Christmas holidays and the last day before the Muscovites returned to work, so the gallery was quite crowded. Even so, I had a sense of being arrested by the stillness of the icon. The three figures are painted close to the viewer and there is virtually no foreground space. It is you and them.

For 500 years the icon had its place in the iconostasis of the church in Sergiev Posad, 44 miles north-east of Moscow. (An iconostasis is a wooden screen made up of icons, separating the sanctuary, where the Eucharist is celebrated, from the nave, where the congregation stands.) Over time, the *olipha*, the covering of varnish, had become blackened by soot from candle flames and dust in the air until little was visible. In earlier centuries, lacking the necessary technique to clean the icon, it was overpainted twice, following the relief of the outline but using darker colours. Later, for protection, it was covered by an *oklad*, a gold and silver metallic sheet, embossed so that only the faces and hands were left visible.

In the early 20th century, however, techniques were developed that enabled icons to be cleaned. In 1905, and again in 1918, restorations took place that removed the *oklad* and cleaned off the overpainting that masked Rublev's work. Though damaged in several places and with barely any gold remaining, the beauty of his original icon was revealed once more. In 1929, the restored icon was placed in the Tretyakov gallery, where it could be protected and where humidity levels could be monitored. Since that time, the icon has gained wide popularity, well beyond the Orthodox Church. Millions of copies have been printed, books have been written and talks given about it, and a procession of admirers, like us, have come to stand and gaze. What exactly is so captivating about it?

In contrast to the intense colours of most other icons, the palette that Rublev chose is cool and fresh. Although faded, it is possible to see tiny amounts of the gold that he laid on as a background and which he used also for the haloes. It is a creamy yellow gold rather than a warm red gold. The blue is made from the mineral lapis lazuli, which is not seen in any other icon of the same period or earlier: Rublev was the first iconographer to use it. Lapis lazuli is found only in the region then called Persia, and it was enormously expensive. Rublev did not use only small touches of it, however; he applied it to large areas, especially in the central angel's mantle. The blue looks effective against the ivory of the haloes, and would have been even more splendid next to the original pale gold. The ivory-coloured table gives a sense of space and the single chalice is accentuated. The pale green of the mantle worn by the angel to the right adds to the fresh effect. The icon is full of light and clarity and such peace that I could have stayed in front of it for a very long time, despite having to share it with many others.

St Sergius of Radonezh

To continue our exploration of the story of Andrei Rublev and his icon of the Trinity, we felt it was important to make a visit to Sergiev Posad (formerly known by the Soviet name of Zagorsk) and to the church in the monastery for which the icon was commissioned.

Two days later, after a fresh fall of snow, we caught a train to Sergiev Posad (*posad* means 'village', so it is 'the village of Sergius'). Our journey into the Russian countryside took us through forests of snow-laden birch and pine, with wooden houses, in faded colours, nestling among the trees. We arrived after about an hour and walked towards the monastery. As it came into view through the bare winter trees, we stopped, involuntarily, at the sight of it. Across a little valley and on the opposite hillside there was a large enclave of gleaming white walls surrounding a tall white cathedral. The building was topped with one gold and four intensely blue onion-shaped cupolas, spangled with golden stars. It was a breathtaking sight in the snowy landscape. This is the Trinity–St Sergius Lavra. '*Lavra*' was originally the name given to a cluster of hermits' cells or caves with a church, but today it is the name given to a high-ranking monastery that has evolved from a hermitage. It was camera-clicking time.

I was fascinated to learn something of the story of St Sergius of Radonezh. Like the name 'Jesus of Nazareth', so 'Sergius of Radonezh' anchors the man in the place where he spent his childhood and youth. He founded the monastery and later became the abbot there. It was in his honour that Rublev painted the icon.

St Sergius could be described as the St Francis of the Russian people, one of their most popular and beloved saints. He was born on 3 May 1314 into a wealthy and influential family (like Francis), and was given the name Bartholomew. Sadly, his parents died when he was still a young man, and, at the age of 23, he and his elder brother Stefan, who was widowed and had become a monk, decided to move away and live as hermits. They built themselves a cell and a small wooden church, which they dedicated to the Holy Trinity, in a clearing on a low hill, surrounded by thick forest in which roamed bears and packs of wolves.

The life of a hermit was very difficult, especially during the harsh Russian winter, when temperatures can drop to as low as minus 40°C. After a while, Stefan felt that he was unable to cope with the scarcity of food and the rigours of the cold, so he left his brother and returned to a monastery in Moscow.

Bartholomew remained on his own for two years in silence and prayer, preparing himself to take his monastic vows. He was given the tonsure of a monk (the shaving of the crown of the head) on 7 October 1342, which is the feast day of two Roman soldiers, Sergius and Bacchus, who were martyred for their Christian faith. It was the practice to take the name of the saint who was celebrated on the day the tonsure was received, and so he adopted the name Sergius. Thereafter, he lived an even more austere life of solitude, reading the Bible, working in his garden and praying unceasingly.

Despite the remote location of his hermitage, word of Sergius' ascetic lifestyle and his piety spread around and monks began to come to him to seek his guidance. They built their own cells and a community was formed. After some time, they persuaded Sergius to become their leader. At first he resisted, preferring to remain an ordinary monk, but eventually he agreed to be ordained to the priesthood and to become the abbot of the monastery. Farmers and city dwellers came for his blessing and then settled in the area, and a nearby *posad* (village) was established, which later grew into the town of Sergiev Posad.

One night, while Sergius was praying, he heard a voice calling his name. He was greatly surprised and opened the window of his cell to see who had summoned him. A miraculous vision appeared—a great light coming from heaven that made the night as bright as day. Once again a voice called him, saying, 'Sergius, you pray for your children and the Lord has heard your prayer. See how many monks have come together in honour of the Holy Trinity and to be guided by you.' Then the saint saw a flock of birds that flew over and around the monastery. The voice said, 'The number of your monks will be as the number of the birds, and even after you, it will not decrease if they choose to follow in your footsteps.'

Although Sergius was abbot of the monastery, in his humility he did not let his position interfere with his life of service. He took the words of Christ as his example: 'The Son of Man came not to be served but to serve' (Matthew 20:28). He officiated at the daily liturgies and spent nights in prayer, but he also prepared food, carried water from the spring (leaving a bucket in each monk's cell), made boots and habits for his brother monks and helped to build the wooden cells for the new arrivals. He himself wore garments that were patched and tattered, so that sometimes those who met him failed to recognise him as the renowned abbot from Radonezh, whose fame was spreading throughout the land. He was asked by Metropolitan Alexius of Moscow to become his successor (the equivalent of an Archbishop in the Western church) but Sergius declined, preferring to remain a simple monk.

Like St Francis, Sergius was a friend to birds and wild animals. There is a story that tells how he regularly fed a bear that came near to his hut. If there was not enough bread for the two of them, he gave his portion to the bear, because, he said, 'the bear does not understand about fasting'.

As a result of his prayers for them, many people were cured and numerous miracles took place, such as the restoration of sight and deliverance from demonic oppression. Gradually he became famous all over the country. On one occasion, Prince Dimitry Donskoy of Moscow came to ask for Sergius' blessing before leading his army to fight the Tatars, so that Russia might be released from the Mongol yoke, which had oppressed and fragmented the people for over 40 years. Sergius was passionate about the need for Russia to be freed and reunified so, although he was non-political and a man of peace, he gave his blessing and predicted the victory that would begin the liberation of Russia. The prince and his army did indeed win a great victory on the Kulikovo Field on 8 September 1380, the first major Russian victory against the Tatars. After that, the Moscow princes became the patrons of the Trinity monastery.

In Sergius' lifetime, eight satellite monasteries were formed (all in all, the disciples of St Sergius have founded about 400 monasteries). Six months before his death, he handed over the responsibility of abbacy to his first disciple, Nikon. He then lived in silence until his death on 25 September 1392 at the age of 78. It was written of him, 'Although the saint did not want glory, neither when he was alive nor after his death, the mighty power of God glorified him. At his departure the angels preceded him to heaven, opening before him the doors of paradise and leading him into the longed for blessing. And what he had always wished, he saw—the illumination of the Most Holy Trinity.'[1]

Thirty years later, in 1422, Sergius was canonised and has become the patron saint of Russia, also fondly known as the Abbot of Russia. His feast days are 25 September (the anniversary of his death) and 5 July, the day his relics were found when the site of the old wooden church was being cleared for rebuilding. Only months after his death, the monastery had been burnt down and destroyed by Tatars. There were successive attacks over the next 30 years, but each time Abbot Nikon insisted that the monastery must be rebuilt. In 1422, the year of Sergius' canonisation, Nikon dismantled the wooden church and instead built a stone church on the site, over the grave of the saint. The church was then designated as a cathedral and dedicated to the Holy Trinity. The building still stands today and contains the saint's relics.

Nikon commissioned the famous painter-monks Andrei Rublev and Daniil Cherny, among others, to paint the church and cover it with frescoes and icons. Andrei painted his Trinity icon in honour of St Sergius, the focus of whose teaching had always been the Trinity. In a climate of fear and dissension in the country, Sergius had believed that contemplation of the Holy Trinity destroys all discord as people let their minds dwell on the unity that exists between the Trinity. It took pride of place to the right of the central Holy Doors in the iconostasis, through which the priests enter the sanctuary to celebrate the Eucharist. Today a copy of Rublev's icon is installed in the same position.

Andrei and Daniil finished their work in 1427, the year in which Abbot Nikon died. He was also later canonised. The two iconographers returned to Moscow and to their community at the Andronikov Monastery. Andrei died only a few years later, on 29 January 1430, and his death was followed closely by that of his friend, Daniil. Andrei Rublev was himself canonised in 1988 by the Russian Orthodox Church. His feast day is celebrated on 29 January, the date of his death, and on 4 July, a date that he shares with St Andrew of Crete.

Over the years, the monastery enclosure of the Trinity–St Sergius Lavra has expanded. It now contains the Trinity Cathedral, the Dormition Cathedral, nine churches, the Tsar's Chambers (which were used by pilgrims from the royal family), the Metropolitan's Chambers, where the Patriarch of Moscow and all Russia stays on his visits to the Lavra, and a bell tower, one of the tallest in Russia. There is also a museum, a refectory, a theological academy and a thick fortified wall punctuated by eleven towers, as well as the living quarters for the brotherhood of monks. The monastery's influence has spread far and wide: it has come a very long way from being just a wooden hut and church in a forest clearing. The Trinity–St Sergius Lavra has long been considered the spiritual centre of Russian Orthodox Christianity.

Stepping inside

As we drew near to the entrance of the monastery on our winter visit, we were met by a large flock of pigeons on the ground. It reminded us of the vision given to St Sergius, in which he saw a flock of birds that was likened to the number of monks who would link themselves to the monastery. A little girl in a gold and red furry coat and hat ran among the birds, sending them swirling up into the sky before they fluttered down to the snowy ground to feed on the seed that was being thrown to them by visitors.

We passed through the entrance, frescoed with scenes from the life of St Sergius, and wandered in the compound, marvelling at the magnificent buildings in pastel shades of yellow, aquamarine, rose and blue. We entered the pale maize-coloured cathedral of the Holy Trinity and stood watching, in the dimly lit interior, the procession of people who had come to light a candle and pay homage to the saint. There was an atmosphere of reverence and holy worship. We gazed at the replica icon of the Trinity and imagined how beautiful Rublev's icon would have appeared in its freshness. Just as it had arrested me at the gallery, it could not have failed to make an impact on the worshippers gathered in the cathedral, centuries before.

Then we returned to Moscow, where we had been invited by a friend of Joanna's to have a meal with her, her elderly mother and her concert pianist son in their flat. A pile of homemade blinis (pancakes), red caviar and sturgeon awaited us. We felt very welcome and enjoyed their open hospitality.

Finally, we paid a visit to the Andronikov Monastery (now a museum of icons) where Andrei and Daniil had lived for many years and where they are both buried. In one of the rooms, an elderly attendant came up and greeted us with a wide smile, eager to offer us information about the icons. Her name was Ella and she was delighted to have an opportunity to practise her English. After a while, she beckoned us to follow her into a tiny staff room under the stairs, where she proceeded to make us a cup of tea and a snack lunch of salami and bread, followed by a delicious homemade chocolate cake. It was another example of spontaneous Russian hospitality, which leads me to the next chapter and the story of Abraham's hospitality on which the icon is based.

– For reflection –

'The Son of Man came not to be served but to serve' (Matthew 20:28).

In what ways are you able to serve others?

What opportunities might you have to offer care and friendship in practical ways?

Chapter 4

The hospitality of Abraham

Before taking time to contemplate Rublev's icon, it is important to look closely at the passage on which it is based—Genesis 18:1–16.

The Lord appeared to Abraham by the oaks of Mamre, as he sat at the entrance of his tent in the heat of the day. He looked up and saw three men standing near him. When he saw them, he ran from the tent entrance to meet them, and bowed down to the ground. He said, 'My lord, if I find favour with you, do not pass by your servant. Let a little water be brought, and wash your feet, and rest yourselves under the tree. Let me bring a little bread, that you may refresh yourselves, and after that you may pass on—since you have come to your servant.' So they said, 'Do as you have said.' And Abraham hastened into the tent to Sarah, and said, 'Make ready quickly three measures of choice flour, knead it, and make cakes.' Abraham ran to the herd, and took a calf, tender and good, and gave it to the servant, who hastened to prepare it. Then he took curds and milk and the calf that he had prepared, and set it before them; and he stood by them under the tree while they ate.

They said to him, 'Where is your wife Sarah?' And he said, 'There, in the tent.' Then one said, 'I will surely return to you in due season, and your wife Sarah shall have a son.' And Sarah was listening at the tent entrance behind him. Now Abraham and Sarah were old, advanced in age; it had ceased to be with

Sarah after the manner of women. So Sarah laughed to herself, saying, 'After I have grown old, and my husband is old, shall I have pleasure?' The Lord said to Abraham, 'Why did Sarah laugh, and say, "Shall I indeed bear a child, now that I am old?" Is anything too wonderful for the Lord? At the set time I will return to you, in due season, and Sarah shall have a son.' But Sarah denied, saying, 'I did not laugh'; for she was afraid. He said, 'Oh yes, you did laugh.'

Then the men set out from there, and they looked towards Sodom; and Abraham went with them to set them on their way.

It is a story of typical Middle Eastern hospitality, both spontaneous and generous. Unexpectedly and at an inconvenient time, three men draw near to Abraham's tent. He is an old man, 99 years of age, sitting at the entrance of his tent in the heat of the day, a time when everything quietens down and people are at rest. Yet as soon as Abraham sees them, instead of ignoring them and continuing his siesta, he gets up hurriedly, walks to meet them and accords them honour by bowing down to the ground before them.

He asks them not to pass by but to stay and be refreshed, and to allow him to serve a meal to them. I notice how many 'immediate' words there are in the passage: 'hurried', 'quick', 'ran'. For an old man, Abraham was sprightly and eager to welcome them.

The aim of Middle Eastern hospitality is that strangers should be welcomed as guests and should leave as friends. There are usually four phases in their cycle of hospitality.

• The initial invitation: It would be an insult to the community not to show hospitality to travellers. Abraham was spontaneous and sincere in his invitation.

- Screening or discerning the intentions of the people wel-comed into the house: Abraham asked no questions, however. He received the men as they were and took them on trust. He washed their feet, which was a sign of acceptance.
- Making provision and offering protection: Abraham laid on a lavish meal for the men and, while they ate, stood nearby at a respectful distance, under the shade of a tree. He offered them a refuge and rest from their travels.
- Departure: It was intended that guests should depart in peace—the Hebrew word *shalom*. Abraham went the extra mile, literally, as 'he walked along with them to see them on their way'.

The actions of Abraham and Sarah are a reminder of the injunction in the letter to the Hebrews: 'Do not neglect to show hospitality to strangers, for by doing that some have entertained angels without knowing it' (13:2).

Abraham and Sarah were richly rewarded for their gener-osity: within a year, their son Isaac was born to them in their old age. In the history of the people of Israel, this encounter would turn out to be a pivotal moment and would eventually lead to the birth of Jesus Christ, the Saviour of the world.

There is another point to notice in this passage. At the outset of the story, the visitors are described as 'three men'. When the conversation about Sarah begins, however, it is no longer three men who speak, but 'the Lord'. The three have become singular, and this is seen as a foreshadowing of the Trinity.

As iconographers were prohibited from depicting the Father and the Spirit, they seized on this story as a symbol of the Trinity and the hospitality at the heart of it. Between

God the Father, God the Son and God the Holy Spirit there is union and communion, and this hospitality is not only given to one another but, remarkably, extended to the world.

Interpretations of the scene

There has been a long, slow development in the painting of this scene from Genesis, and Rublev's icon is the culmination of that development. The earliest depiction is probably a fresco found in a catacomb on the Via Latina, an ancient road that leads south-east from Rome. The fresco is thought to have been painted in the first half of the fourth century. In it, a bearded Abraham, sitting under a tree, raises his hand in welcome to three young men, dressed in white, who return the gesture of blessing. Next to Abraham is a calf, giving a hint of the hospitality to come.

In the fifth century, the scene appears in the magnificent mosaics in the churches of Santa Maria Maggiore, Rome, and in San Vitale, Ravenna. At this point, the three visitors have all acquired haloes or nimbi, denoting their supernatural qualities. There is very little differentiation between them, although the central figure might be seen as slightly prominent. By the 13th century, the figures are clearly depicted as angels, having wings as well as haloes, and can be seen in the cathedrals of Monreale, Sicily and San Marco in Venice.

All of the representations mentioned come from the Latin Church of the West but when, in the eleventh century, the Byzantine Church of the East took up the theme of the hospitality of Abraham, a new style emerged. The central angel is often larger than the others; he may have a scroll in his left hand, while his right hand is raised in blessing.

The colour of his clothing is often differentiated from the other two; the mark of a cross appears on his halo and, in many cases, above him is the inscription 'IC XC', the Greek abbreviation for Jesus Christ. The scene also contains the figures of Abraham and Sarah, the calf and possibly a servant, as well as the house, the tree and the rock in the background, making the tableau somewhat cluttered. Although the figures on either side of the central figure are shown as heavenly messengers with no personal distinguishing features, the title 'The Holy Trinity' began to be used.

Theophanes was a significant icon painter. He lived from 1370 to 1405; as his name suggests, he was Greek, but he worked in Russia. His frescoes in the Church of the Transfiguration of Christ, Novgorod, are exceptionally fine, and he established schools of painting in both Novgorod and Moscow. A certain young man, Andrei Rublev by name, was among his assistants in Moscow. Theophanes painted a fresco of the hospitality of Abraham for the church in Novgorod with the title 'The Trinity', and Rublev would have been aware of it.

The icon that may have influenced Rublev most of all, however, was to be found in the former wooden church of St Sergius' Trinity Monastery at Sergiev Posad, the very monastery for whose new stone church Rublev's depiction of the Holy Trinity was later commissioned. Like Rublev's own icon, it is painted on a large scale (63 inches by 48 inches), in contrast to many Greek and Russian depictions of the tableau. It was painted around 1411 by an unknown iconographer and now hangs in the Sergiev Posad museum. There is the same inclination of the angels' heads and similar clothing as in Rublev's icon, but Abraham and Sarah are still visible and there are three chalices on the table.[1]

As I have said, little is known about Andrei Rublev as a man, in contrast to his reputation as a painter. We know that he became a monk and we get glimpses of him occasionally in the writings of those who chronicled life in his monastery, one of whom was St Joseph of Volokalamsk (1440–1515). He describes Andrei and his fellow iconographer, Daniil, as being fully committed to the monastic way of life, to fasting and to prayer. They were grounded in God's love and had no care for earthly things. If they were not occupied with icon painting themselves, they would sit in front of other icons and contemplate them without distraction until they were filled with a divine joy and radiance, evident to those around them through their composure and shining faces.

Describing Rublev's icon of the Trinity, Ouspensky writes, 'This icon with its inexhaustible content, its harmonious equilibrium of composition, majestically calm figures of the angels, light, joyous summer colours could be the creation only of a man who had stilled in his soul all agitation and doubt and was illumined by the light of the knowledge of God.'[2]

Rublev must have spent a long time in prayer and thought before painting his icon because, when he eventually came to paint the scene, he took some very bold steps. He made the conscious decision to eliminate the figures of Abraham and Sarah, leaving only the three angels, as his idea was not to illustrate the story but rather to convey the idea of the Trinity. He gave all the angels equal importance and, while keeping the historical elements of the event by depicting the tree, the portico of a house and the mountain in the background, he reduced the content to a minimum, thus creating a sense of space and peace. Harmony is achieved through the circular movement between the three angels and their inclination towards one another—but more of this in the next chapter, when we will take time to contemplate this magnificent icon in detail.

As I have written the preceding chapters, it has felt like the process of preparing the board on which an icon is to be painted. It has involved developing my awareness of the history of icon painting, the techniques used in creating the images, the context in which Rublev's icon came into being, and the biblical passage that is used to illustrate the Holy Trinity. Now it is really time for 'the long look'.

～ For reflection ～

We have a framed piece of calligraphy hanging by the front door of our home. It was written and given to us by our son as a Christmas present a few years ago. He has taken a sentence from the Rule of Benedict—no. 653, which is based on Matthew 25:35. It reads, 'All guests who present themselves are to be welcomed as Christ; for he himself will say "I was a stranger and you welcomed me."'

I find this challenging. In my encounters with other people, do I sincerely welcome friends, nodding acquaintances and strangers? It means making space for them in my heart, listening to them, serving them as best as I can. It involves taking a risk because, in our stressed society today, I don't know whether or not my offer will be accepted.

Take time to reflect on your own hospitality towards others. What might it feel like to be on the receiving end of your welcome?

One of my favourite verses occurs in John's Gospel and relates to the hospitality that is offered to us by the Trinity of love. Jesus said,

'Abide in me as I abide in you' (John 15:4)—in other words, 'Make your home in me and I will make mine in you.'

You may like to write down what 'home' means to you. Is that also true of your relationship with God?

~ Chapter 5 ~

The circle of love

In the Orthodox Church, icons of the Trinity are particularly associated with the feast of Pentecost, which celebrates the outpouring of the Holy Spirit and the beginning of the Church's mission. The apostles and those with them, who received the Holy Spirit, knew God as Creator; in Jesus Christ they had seen the Son of God and now, with the coming of God the Holy Spirit, the revelation of the Trinity was complete.

At that festival, the church is decorated with branches of trees, fresh greenery and flowers. The festival of Pentecost is of Old Testament origin: it celebrated the giving of the law to Moses on Mount Sinai and was also a thanksgiving for the first fruits of the earth. The greenery is also seen as a symbol of the new life that the Holy Spirit causes to grow in us. An icon of the Trinity is the focal point as the worshippers listen to the liturgy and the hymns. I can imagine that it would be a deeply moving experience, with the visual element giving extra significance to the spoken word. That is the rightful setting for an icon, as they were never intended to be private devotional pictures or to hang in galleries. They are designed to be at the heart of a worshipping community.

Rublev's icon may no longer be in its intended place but it has touched the lives of many who have spent time in prayer before it. It draws us in and makes space for us to encounter God in a deep but gentle way. Below, I will share some of the things I have seen after looking at the icon for a long time. As you gaze at it, I am sure you will see more.

The long look

As you come to contemplate the icon, I suggest that you set aside some time when you won't be interrupted and find a quiet space where you can sit comfortably. You might like to light a candle or play some soft music to help you quieten down and settle.

Be patient and prepared to take unhurried time. Let the icon serve as a bridge into prayer and the worship of God.

Here is a suggested prayer to say before you read further:

Lord, open my eyes that I may behold your glory;
draw me into the mystery of the Trinity
and into the circle of love.
This I ask in the name of the Father and of the Son and of the
Holy Spirit.
Amen

In this icon, we are not only looking at three angels but at the Trinity and at the harmony and love that exist between them. Each of the figures possesses the whole fullness of the Godhead, and so Rublev has deliberately given them similar faces, figures and hairstyles, differentiating them only by their clothing.

- The three angels have equal importance.
- There is a sense of history but also a timeless quality about them.
- Their faces are youthful, yet there is a quiet maturity.
- They are neither male nor female.
- Their haloes depict their holiness.
- The stave that each one holds gives them authority. It also signifies that they were messengers in the biblical story.

- They are similar and yet different.
- Each one of them lives for the others. They are in eternal communion.
- They give the impression of perfect unity. Their wings, which seem to form an enclosing curtain, emphasise the bond between them, echoing Jesus' prayer to his Father: '... that they may be one, as we are one' (John 17:11).
- As you gaze at the icon, there is both rest and movement. There is the sense of a moment frozen in time, of movement and conversation arrested. Their stillness draws us into stillness.

Rublev was the first iconographer to use a circle in his design—the symbol of perfection, unity and eternity, having no beginning and no ending. The circle is created by the three figures, which, unusually, are all the same size. In other icons, the central figure is larger, representing the Son, with a smaller angel on either side. In Rublev's icon, the similarity in size of the figures draws attention to the fact that they are of equal importance. We could draw an imaginary circle around the outside of their bodies and another in the centre of the picture, following the inner curve.

Very often, in other icons, the three figures sit in a line facing the viewer. Here, however, because of the curve of their bodies and the inclination of their heads, the movement flows in an anti-clockwise direction. Even the tree and the mountain in the background echo the movement, which would be arrested by the upright house behind the figure on the left if it were not for the inclination of the head, which leads our gaze around the circle again. The movement goes around and around and, as it is impossible to make full-face contact with the figures, their gaze draws us on: there is no place for our eye to stop.

Imagining the picture in three dimensions, we can also see a flattened circle extending out towards us—like a table top. But there is a space in the circle: if I, as the viewer, step into the space that is offered, I enter the circle—the circle of love.

Rublev uses two triangular shapes in his design. One has its apex at the head of the central figure and the other is inverted, with its apex at the bottom centre of the painting. Together they create a star shape.

An octagon can also be found in what is called the 'sacred geometry'. This means the shape that you get from combining all the other shapes—the circle, the six-pointed star and the cross (which we will discover later). For early Christians, eight was the number that symbolised the formation of the new covenant. It marked the seven days of creation—six of work and the seventh day of rest—plus an eighth day for the resurrection of Jesus. Early Byzantine churches were built in the form of octagons, and it is said that archaeologists were able to identify the apostle Peter's house in Capernaum because it contained an octagonal building within it, which would have been used as a place of worship.

The octagon, as a symbol not only of resurrection but also of regeneration, has a close association with baptism. Fonts are often octagonal in shape and the baptismal cross has eight points—a combination of the Greek cross with the Greek letter X, the first initial of the title of Christ.

Rublev chose a palette of pure gold and tones of gold, azure blue and moss green for the tree, and a fresh green for the figure on the right. The central figure adds depth to the painting, being clothed in deep red, blue and a band of gold. The figure on the left wears garments of the softest brown and pink. The staves in the figures' hands are thin lines of vermilion. The light that shines around their heads is ivory in colour, although originally it would have been gold to express the glory of God. Ivory white is used for the altar, the place of sacrificial offering. Blue is the colour that is common to all three figures, the colour of heaven and a symbol of divinity in iconographic language.

In this icon, heaven touches earth. In Stephen's speech to the Sanhedrin in Acts 7, where he outlines all that God has done in redeeming his people, he quotes from a prophetic saying that God does not live in temples made with hands. The whole world is his temple in which he is present everywhere: for 'heaven is [his] throne', in which he rests, 'and the earth is [his] footstool' (v. 49), over which he rules. This icon gives me a strong impression that the Trinity is seated in the heavenly realms but with a footstool on earth. Rublev has even painted the ground beneath their feet in green.

When he painted the icon, Rublev would have added in the names of the three figures but, with the passage of time, the damage to the icon and the overpainting processes, the names have been lost. There is some debate as to whether the central figure is God the Father or Christ the Son, although there is a huge weight of opinion to support the latter suggestion. This would mean that the figures appear in order, as in the doxology (a short hymn of praise to the Trinity) and in the creed: 'I believe in God the Father, God the Son and God the Holy Spirit.' Also, as I have mentioned, in earlier icons the central figure was positively identified as Christ with 'IX IC' written above, so that is how I have chosen to read Rublev's version. We should remember, though, that there is no clearly designated 'correct' way: we are left free to interpret as we will.

As we remain in silence before the icon, we can trust the

Holy Spirit to lead us into worship, not of the icon but of the Godhead that it portrays.

When I stood in front of it at the Tretyakov Gallery, I became aware not only of love between the Trinity, but also of sorrow. The line that came to my mind was 'Did e'er such love and sorrow meet?' from the hymn 'When I survey the wondrous cross'. It was as if I could see the Father commissioning the Son to offer himself as a sacrifice for the salvation of the world. There is a sense of Jesus the Son saying, 'My Father, if it is possible, let this cup pass from me; yet not what I want but what you want' (Matthew 26:39). His head is bent in submission but his obedience gives no pleasure to the Father; rather, there is a quiet but firm resolve. They are all in agreement. At great cost, especially to the Son, the triune Godhead is united in the plan of salvation for the world, and that plan includes me:

For God so loved the world that he gave his only Son, so that everyone who believes in him may not perish but may have eternal life. Indeed, God did not send the Son into the world to condemn the world, but in order that the world might be saved through him. (John 3:16–17)

Although the Father, Son and Holy Spirit are of one essence, nevertheless there are individual distinctions, and Rublev makes that wonderfully plain to see.

God the Holy Spirit

We will start following the movement around the circle with the figure on the right, the Holy Spirit. He is the one who leads us in and interprets the life of God to us. He is dressed in a blue tunic with a gorgeous light-green mantle, probably painted in *terre verte* pigment, otherwise known as 'green earth'. Green is the liturgical colour of Pentecost in the Orthodox Church and the symbolic colour of the Holy Spirit. The Spirit, who breathes life, wears colours that speak of creation. Blue reminds us of sky and water; green speaks of vegetation. All living things owe their freshness to his touch.

Flying in over England when returning from a hot, dry country, I become aware of the vibrant, fresh green of the countryside. It is the effect of an island climate, where rain is plentiful and everything looks very lush. In early May, I often walk with friends in bluebell woods. The delicate lime-green unfolding leaves of the beech trees hang above the carpet of scented blue flowers. There is the same freshness in the way that Rublev has chosen to dress the Spirit, and it complements the figure's youthful appearance.

His is the only stave that is seen in its full length, as if it is pointing towards earth. His hand gives the impression of not only blessing the cup of sacrifice but also of indicating downwards, for he is the one who breathes the life of God into us. His action is to transform us and it is through him that we are invited to experience new life in Christ.

Above the Spirit is a mountain. Maybe the mountain represents faith, a gift of the Holy Spirit or the meeting places where God revealed his glory, such as Mount Sinai, where he appeared to Moses, or the mount of transfiguration, where Jesus was seen in glory by three of his disciples.

As the icon is based on the story of Abraham, however, perhaps the mountain represents Mount Moriah, on which Isaac, the promised son in the story, would be offered for sacrifice—Abraham's response to a test that God devised to prove his faith. The story is recorded in Genesis 22 and it is a foreshadowing of the greater story of the triune God's self-sacrificing love in the giving of the Son to be our Saviour.

The curvature of the body and the bowed head of the figure on the right draw us into the circle and lead us towards the central figure, whom I have taken to be Christ the Son. The Spirit does not let us stay with himself. His work is to reveal God the Father through God the Son.

God the Son

The Son of God is dressed in a robe of reddish brown, the colour of earth, denoting his humanity. He has a kingly band of gold across his shoulder and a mantle of blue is draped over him as a sign of his divinity. His robes convey the fact that in his person he unites heaven and earth. There is almost an equal amount of blue and brown, perhaps denoting his dual nature: the divine and the human meet in him. This is Jesus Christ, God incarnate, sent by the Father to be the redeemer of the world. It is interesting to note that his mantle is worn in such a way that his right arm is free, whereas the left arm of the Spirit is free. Perhaps this refers to the teaching of the early Fathers of the Church, such as Irenaeus, Bishop of Lyons (c.130–c.202), that the Son and the Spirit are the two 'hands' of the Father, through which he does his work.

Two fingers of the Son's right hand are extended in a gesture of blessing over the cup of sacrifice. If you take a ring, perhaps a wedding ring, and look at the icon through it, you will see that the hand of Christ is the central point of the outer circle. The Genesis story tells us that Abraham killed a fatted calf to feed his guests, and the chalice on the table contains a calf's head. This is a prototype of the sacrificial offering that Christ would make of himself, and the chalice is being blessed by the one who was himself the Lamb of God, the sin offering.

It was only after I had gazed at the icon for some considerable time that I noticed the shape that frames Christ. It is formed by the inner line of the figures on either side and it is the shape of a chalice, an embodiment of his words at the Last Supper: 'This is my body, which is given for you... This cup that is poured out for you is the new covenant in my blood' (Luke 22:19–20).

Above the Son's head is a tree, which represents the oaks of Mamre in the story of Abraham. As Rublev would know, however, the tree has other connotations. It could represent the tree of life, as mentioned in Revelation 22:2. It could stand for the tree of the knowledge of good and evil that grew in the garden of Eden (Genesis 2:9). It could also represent the cross, for, just as a tree was linked with our downfall, so it is also linked with our salvation in Christ. Irenaeus, Bishop of Lyons, wrote, 'Just as through a tree we became God's debtors, so through a tree we receive the cancellation of our debts.'[1]

Peter writes in his first letter, '[Christ] himself bore our sins in his body on the tree, that we might die to sin and live to righteousness' (1 Peter 2:24).

If you trace an imaginary line from the tree, down through the fingers of Christ's hand, the chalice and the box shape at the front of the altar, and if you trace another line across the heads of the figures either side of Christ, you end up with a cross. There is no circle without the cross; no eternal life without death; no heavenly kingdom without Calvary.

If you cover the head of Christ in the icon, it looks as if he should be looking forward, straight at you, but in fact his head is turned, directing its gaze of love and obedience towards the receptive figure on the left, God the Father. In life, Jesus always attributed glory to his Father and he lived in perfect obedience to his Father's will: 'Jesus said to them, "Very truly, I tell you, the Son can do nothing on his own, but only what he sees the Father doing; for whatever the Father does, the Son does likewise. The Father loves the Son and shows him all that he himself is doing"' (John 5:19–20).

God the Father

The Father, the slightest of the three figures, has an air of mystery about him. Over his blue garment he wears a shimmering, irridescent robe in pink and brown, shot through with hues of blue and green. It gives him an ethereal appearance. This is how it should be, for Jesus said, '[No one] has seen the Father except the one who is from God; he has seen the Father' (John 6:46). It is Jesus who makes the Father known to us. So, in the icon, his tender look towards the Father bridges the gap that we might otherwise experience in relationship with the Father, who is both love and mystery.

The Father's gaze is turned toward the other two but his head is not as inclined. He receives the acknowledgment by the Son and Holy Spirit that he is their source and origin— the doctrine held by the Orthodox Church. Yet, in directing his gaze back at them, he contributes to the circular motion.

The Father exists to give life eternally to the Son and to the Holy Spirit. The Son and the Spirit are living because they, in turn, give themselves to the Father. Each person of the Trinity lives only for the others in perfect interdependence, and so the Father too blesses the cup of sacrifice and the mission that his Son will accomplish.

Above the Father's head is a house with an open door. This symbolises Abraham's dwelling, although, in fact, he lived in a tent. In the deeper meaning of the icon, it may refer to the Church or to the words of Jesus, 'In my Father's house there are many dwelling-places' (John 14:2).

As I write, a copy of the icon is in front of me and I have noticed once again that, mirroring the inclination of the two figures they accompany, both the mountain and the tree lean towards the upright house. Perhaps it signifies that one day there will be a consummation of all things in the eternal home of the Father. As David writes in his psalm, 'I will dwell in the house of the Lord for ever' (Psalm 23:6, NIV).

What's wonderful about this icon is that you can always see more meaning in it. Every detail was prayerfully and carefully thought out by Rublev. Nothing was accidental; everything he painted was for a divine purpose.

A space at the table

The cubed table or altar at the centre of the icon is both the place of Abraham's hospitality, given to the angels in the Genesis story, and God's place of hospitality that he generously offers to us. The Trinity is not in an exclusive relationship, and we should notice that there is a space left open on our side of the table so that we can join in.

Look again at the icon and you will notice a small rectangle in the altar front, which seems to sit awkwardly with the flowing movement of the overall design. There are several possible explanations for this rectangle. It could represent the four corners of the earth, because, at the time when the icon was painted, people still believed that the world was flat. It could be the place in an altar where the relics of martyrs were deposited—people who laid down their lives for Christ, who had sacrificed his life for them. Alternatively, it could be the place where the reserved elements for the Eucharist were kept—consisting, in the Orthodox Church, of bread with a drop of consecrated wine on it.

Each of these explanations has one factor in common: they are all connected in some way with us, the people of this world. They are, in different ways, an invitation to come to the table.

I find this icon a helpful image to hold in my mind when I come to receive Communion, for if I take that place at the table, I complete the circle. I am then faced with the figure opposite to me—Christ, the Son of God—and he is blessing the cup of sacrifice. I am faced with his redeeming love for me. I take the bread and drink from the cup, humbled and deeply grateful.

Henri Nouwen writes:

The more we look at this holy image with the eyes of faith, the more we come to realise that it is painted not as a lovely decoration for a convent church, nor as a helpful explanation of a difficult doctrine, but as a holy place to enter and stay within.

As we place ourselves in front of the icon in prayer, we come to experience a gentle invitation to participate in the intimate conversation that is taking place among the three divine angels and to join them around the table. The movement from the Father toward the Son and the movement of both the Son and the Spirit

toward the Father, become a movement in which the one who prays
is lifted up and held secure.[2]

‑ For reflection ‑

Love bade me welcome, yet my soul drew back,
   Guilty of dust and sin.
But quick-eyed Love, observing me grow slack
   From my first entrance in,
Drew nearer to me, sweetly questioning,
   If I lacked anything.

'A guest,' I answered, 'worthy to be here.'
   Love said, 'You shall be he.'
'I, the unkind, ungrateful? Ah, my dear,
   I cannot look on thee.'
Love took my hand, and smiling, did reply,
   'Who made the eyes but I?'

'Truth, Lord, but I have marred them: let my shame
   Go where it doth deserve.'
'And know you not,' says Love, 'who bore the blame?'
   'My dear, then I will serve.'
'You must sit down,' says Love, 'and taste my meat.'
   So I did sit and eat.[3]
GEORGE HERBERT (1593–1633)

The table is spread, the door is open and the Spirit says, 'Come.'

What does it feel like to join the circle of love?

What response does it provoke in you?

– Chapter 6 –

Exploring the Trinity

After spending time looking at Rublev's icon, my journey leads me to think more about the Trinity. In common with many others, I have never found it an easy concept to grasp. I am not a theologian but these are my thoughts after praying, reading the scriptures (especially John's Gospel) and researching what others have written on the subject. How do you begin to define something that is, in the end, mystery, well beyond the finite mind? As Alister McGrath puts it:

Although we speak of 'the doctrine of the Trinity', what we really mean is the magnificent vision of God that transcends our capacity to understand, describe and explain what is tersely and inadequately summarised by this doctrine. When confronted with the mystery of God, the human mind struggles to take in something that vastly exceeds its capacity to understand. It finds itself overwhelmed by the majesty of God, sometimes reduced to silence, at others trying to put into words what it experiences, while knowing its words fail utterly to express what has been discovered to be true.[1]

The word 'Trinity' is not used in the Bible. The New Testament speaks only of God the Father, Jesus Christ the Son of God and the Holy Spirit, and of the relationship between them. The word 'Trinity' began to be applied to them in the course of later theological reflection. It comes from the Latin word *trinitas*, which means 'threeness', and the first recorded use of the word in reference to the Father, Son and Holy Spirit comes from the pen of Tertullian, a third-century theologian.

While scripture does not contain an explicit doctrine of the Trinity, it does demand that God is understood in a trinitarian way.

- The Bible teaches that there is only one God.
- It also teaches that there are three distinct persons called God, known as the Father, Son and Holy Spirit.
- Therefore, the three persons—Father, Son and Holy Spirit —are one God.
- God is three in one and one in three.

There are also two aspects of God. First, there is his 'transcendence'. This means that he is beyond our knowledge and our imagining: he is Mystery.

There is also the 'immanence' of God: he is the one who comes to us. He is a self-revealing, self-communicating, self-giving God who is totally committed to us and desires to make himself known to us. We see examples of this throughout the Old Testament in his dealings with his chosen people, Israel. Ultimately, we see it in the New Testament, for the love that burned within the heart of the Trinity, and the desire to be in relationship with humankind, led to a truly amazing, even scandalous plan. God himself would become human: he would take on our nature and live within the limitations of the human condition. In this way, he could be touched, seen, heard by us, and we could respond to him. Our brokenness could be healed and we could be brought into a new and living relationship with God the Father, God the Son and God the Holy Spirit.

Paul puts it succinctly in his letter to the Christians at Ephesus: '... one God and Father of all, who is above all and through all and in all' (Ephesians 4:6).

There is God, who is beyond everything, the origin of all that is; but, through Jesus, there is God who is with us, 'Emmanuel'. Then, through the Holy Spirit, there is God who is within us.

In my experience, I am most aware of the immanence of God at times when I am least in control—times of difficulty and uncertainty. I suppose it happens when I am not so full of 'me' and when I am not self-sufficient. Then God has an opportunity to reveal himself as the intimate Emmanuel. I think back to the time when our first child, a little girl, died at the age of 17 months. Yes, Paul and I were deeply sad, but I can also say that we have never, before or since, experienced the presence and comfort of God in such a tangible way as at that time, even amidst our tears. God also chose to reveal himself to us through the love and support of others.

I was aware of God, too, at a time of uncertainty. For 26 years we had used our home as a retreat house and a centre for creativity. When we retired and moved to our present home, after all the activity of 'nest building' I hit a period of depression. I was unsure of my identity without my former context. What could I do in the remaining years of my life? I had a very strong sense of God telling me to do nothing but to enjoy the present period of rest and to wait until a new opportunity for service opened up, without having to look for it. At first, it was strange to have time on my hands and no project to be involved in. Gradually, though, I relaxed into it and decided to inform myself about subjects that interested me. I have a love of nature so I read up about trees, ladybirds, fungi, wildlife in hedgerows and so on. A few months later, a letter arrived: 'out of the blue', I was presented with an opportunity to be involved with BRF and lead Quiet Days for them, which, in turn, has led to this book being written. God made himself known to me when I felt unsure and a bit lost.

With regard to the experience of God's infinite nature, that happens for me when I listen to a sublime piece of music, stand under a night sky studded with stars, gaze at a range of snowclad mountains or watch the sun set over the sea. At those moments, I feel overwhelmed by the greatness of God.

At the heart of the Trinity there is community. No wonder, then, that we, who have been created in the image of God, are relational people with a need to belong and a desire to give and receive love. The relationship between the Trinity is based on love and reciprocity, and this is wonderfully conveyed in Rublev's icon.

The Trinity in action

The Trinity is not just a concept or an idea. It is a way of being. The Father, Son and Holy Spirit are one in essence, yet diverse in their expression of the Godhead, each having their own identity and role to play.

No analogy is adequate to describe the Trinity, and what follows has its limitations, but imagine that you are sitting in a concert hall. You are listening to Dame Kiri Te Kanawa singing a glorious hymn of praise, perhaps Mozart's *Laudate Dominum*, accompanied by a full orchestra. If you separate the music into its constituent parts, you have Mozart as composer, the conductor, orchestra and Dame Kiri as the performers, and then the sound waves that transmit the music to your ears.

Perhaps God the Father is like Mozart the composer. He is the initiator, the one who makes plans, the one who puts everything together and sends his Son to become one of us.

Jesus, the Son, is like the performers. He is the one who responds, the one who is sent and the one who carries out the Father's plan.

The Holy Spirit, God's agent or transmitter, is like the sound waves. He enables us to hear and enter into the experience of the music.

Together, the Trinity make a heavenly music. If we are open, we can be caught up into the experience of it—into the life that God offers.

Of course, the analogy of the Trinity and the concert is a frail one because Mozart is not in Dame Kiri; nor is the orchestra in Mozart. They are separate components working together to produce fine music, whereas the Father is in the Son, the Son is in the Father, the Father and the Son are in the Spirit, and the Spirit is in the Father and the Son. They permeate one another. They are truly one.

The challenge to our understanding is that the three persons of the Trinity are in union with one another, yet they are differentiated. The Father is not the Son and the Son is not the Father. Within the being of one God, the Son does not send; he is sent. It is the Son who is incarnate, crucified and resurrected, not the Father.

It is the Father who initiates and the Son who responds and obeys that initiative. The Father's initiation is fruitful only through the Son's response to it and the Son's response is entirely defined by the Father's initiative.

Reading chapters 5 to 8 of John's Gospel, I find this truth reiterated time after time. In fact, there are 20 instances when Jesus speaks of 'the Father who sent me'. For example, we read that he said, 'I have come down from heaven, not to do my own will, but the will of him who sent me' (John 6:38); 'My teaching is not mine but his who sent me' (7:16); 'When you have lifted up the Son of Man, then you will realise that I am he, and that I do nothing on my own, but I speak these things as the Father instructed me. And the one who sent me is with me; he has not left me alone, for I always do what is pleasing to him' (8:28–29).

The Trinity works together and in harmony. We have specific glimpses of the collaboration of the Trinity through the Scriptures.

The Trinity was there in the act of creation:

In the beginning God created the heavens and the earth. Now the earth was formless and empty, darkness was over the surface of the deep, and the Spirit of God was hovering over the waters. (Genesis 1:1–2, NIV)

Paul writes in his letter to the Colossians:

Christ is the image of the invisible God, the firstborn of all creation; for in him all things in heaven and on earth were created, things visible and invisible, whether thrones or dominions or rulers or powers—all things have been created through him and for him. (1:15–16)

The divine community is evident at the annunciation and in the birth of Jesus Christ:

In the sixth month the angel Gabriel was sent by God to a town in Galilee called Nazareth, to a virgin... [whose] name was Mary... The angel said to her, 'Do not be afraid, Mary, for you have found favour with God. And now, you will conceive in your womb and bear a son, and you will name him Jesus. He will be great, and will be called the Son of the Most High... The Holy Spirit will come upon you, and the power of the Most High will overshadow you; therefore the child to be born will be holy; he will be called Son of God.' (Luke 1:26–27, 30–32, 35)

The three distinct expressions of the Trinity are seen and heard at the baptism of Jesus:

Now when all the people were baptised, and when Jesus also had been baptised and was praying, the heaven was opened, and the Holy Spirit descended on him in bodily form like a dove. And a voice came from heaven, 'You are my Son, the Beloved; with you I am well pleased.' (Luke 3:21–22)

The Trinity is referred to in the ministry of Jesus, when he says to the Pharisees:

'But if it is by the Spirit of God that I cast out demons, then the kingdom of God has come to you.' (Matthew 12:28)

In the events of the transfiguration, we read:

Jesus took with him Peter and James and his brother John and led them up a high mountain, by themselves. And he was transfigured before them, and his face shone like the sun, and his clothes became dazzling white... A bright cloud overshadowed them, and from the cloud a voice said, 'This is my Son, the Beloved; with him I am well pleased; listen to him!' (Matthew 17:1–2, 5)

At the crucifixion of Jesus, the Father, Son and Holy Spirit were all intimately involved in this act of suffering, sacrificial love:

In Christ God was reconciling the world to himself. (2 Corinthians 5:19)

The doctrine of the Trinity is encapsulated when Jesus instructs the apostles before his ascension:

'Go therefore and make disciples of all nations, baptising them

in the name of the Father and of the Son and of the Holy Spirit.'
(Matthew 28:19)

Peter, in his sermon on the day of Pentecost, speaks in the power of the Holy Spirit of God's involvement:

'This man, handed over to you according to the definite plan and foreknowledge of God, you crucified and killed by the hands of those outside the law. But God raised him up, having freed him from death.' (Acts 2:23–24)

Paul, in his letter to the Romans, puts it this way:

If the Spirit of him who raised Jesus from the dead dwells in you, he who raised Christ from the dead will give life to your mortal bodies also through his Spirit that dwells in you. (8:11)

The initiating love of the Father is incarnated by the responsive love of the Son and made real in our lives by the transforming action of the Spirit. This adds up to mutual interdependence so that one can be effective only in coordination with the others.

The divine dance

I have recently been introduced to the word *perichoresis*, and this dynamic, relational concept of the Trinity has excited me. *Perichoresis* came into use in the sixth century but, in the eighth century, John of Damascus (c.675–c.749, often regarded as the last of the Greek Fathers) became best known for his use of the word as an explanation of the Trinity. *Peri* means 'around' (as in 'perimeter'); *choreio* means 'to move' (it is the stem of the word 'choreography'); so *perichoresis* means 'to move around'. John of Damascus said that a dance takes place at the centre of God, where Father, Son and Holy Spirit move around and between one another. They serve each other, give themselves to one another, receive from one another and take mutual delight in one another. There is a movement towards one another and a movement from one another.

The concept of *perichoresis* was translated into the phrase 'the divine dance'. It refers to the mutual indwelling and interpenetration of the Trinity and it is based on words spoken by Jesus: 'I am in the Father and the Father is in me' (John 14:11). On another occasion Jesus said, 'The Father and I are one' (10:30). I like to think of this as a divine entanglement— an interweaving.

In God there is life, relationship, vitality, movement. At the heart of God there is a divine dance, twisting, turning and circling with eternal life. Father, Son and Holy Spirit move and flow and draw life from one another in a bond of perfect love.

I see this 'divine dance' in the circular motion in Rublev's icon. The three figures are motionless and yet also in a graceful movement, which could be described as a dance. They are caught in the act of giving and receiving love as the dance of relationship passes from one to the other, first in one direction, then in the other, on and on. In the dance of love, the Son cries, 'Abba, Father!' and the Father cries, 'My Son' and the love that leaps between them is the Holy Spirit – the Spirit of God himself, for God is Spirit and God is love. Through their dance of love the glory of God is revealed to us.

Have you ever joined in the dance 'The Dashing White Sergeant'? It is a reel, which is a lively Scottish country dance, and it is for sets of three. A man stands between two women, opposite a woman standing between two men. The dance begins as the two sets bow to one another. Holding hands, they dance round in a circle for eight steps and back again. Then, in the sets of three, they dance round one another, weaving in and out, in a figure of eight. Finally, each set of three takes hands and approaches the opposite set, says farewell and moves on to a new set of three to begin the reel again. The dance alternates between 'we are one' and 'we are three'.

In the divine dance we can sense the Trinity acting as one and also as three. As in the reel, there are times of hand-holding solidarity and other times of interweaving. The idea of *perichoresis* dispels the notion of three static beings and instead offers us a doctrine of perfect interrelatedness, a community of light, love and dynamism.

There are several movements in this holy dance. First, there are the three persons of the Trinity moving around and between one another. Then they open the dance out to the world, in the coming of Jesus to be our Saviour and in the sending of the Spirit to make him known to us. The movement is also reversed because, as the Spirit is at work in the world, bringing the truth of the gospel of Christ to us, we respond and turn to God in penitence and faith. Moved by the Spirit, we come to the Father through Christ the Son. We are gathered into God's kingdom and then we in turn, moved by the Spirit, go out to others with the good news of the kingdom. There is a continual ebb and flow, like the tides of the sea; there is a dance going on and we are invited to join in.

~ For reflection ~

Read slowly through John 14 and 15 and look for ways in which the Father, Son and Holy Spirit interrelate and interact with one another. For example, at the beginning of chapter 14, Jesus comforts his disciples, who are distressed about his impending departure, by directing their thoughts towards his Father's house, where one day they will be with him and with his Father. In verse 26, Jesus speaks of all three members of the Trinity, who, after his death, will be at work in the lives of the disciples, teaching them and reminding them of all that Jesus said to them. As a result, we have the Gospels to read and treasure.

Take some time to let God lead you into the wonder and mystery of the Trinity. You may like to choose one of the ways suggested below.

Gaze at the icon; bring yourself once again into the space at the table and allow yourself to be drawn into the love, harmony and movement that flow between the Godhead.

Reflect on an image from nature, such as water. You could fill a bowl or glass with water and think about its life-giving properties and the different forms that water can take—liquid, ice and steam. Think of Jesus' words to the Samaritan woman at the well: 'Those who drink of the water that I will give them will never be thirsty. The water that I will give will become in them a spring of water gushing up to eternal life' (John 4:14). Have a drink and be aware that, just as the water is assimilated into your body, so through faith the life of God can be taken into us.

Be creative: you may like to write a poem or a piece of prose, or use paints to express in colour something of the wonder of God.

Listen to a piece of music that inspires you. Let the sound wash over you and open yourself to the presence of God—Father, Son and Holy Spirit.

– Chapter 7 –

Joining in the dance

As I reflected on the idea of the divine dance, I was reminded of the words of Sydney Carter's well-known hymn, 'Lord of the Dance', which envisages the incarnate Christ as a piper who is calling people to follow him:

Dance, then, wherever you may be,
I am the Lord of the Dance, said he,
And I'll lead you all, wherever you may be,
And I'll lead you all in the Dance, said he.

The last two lines of the hymn are an overwhelming invitation to be caught up into the life, the dance of God: 'I'll live in you if you'll live in me—I am the Lord of the Dance, said he.'[1]

This poetic expression of Christ living in us and us in him echoes John 14:19–20, where Jesus says, 'Because I live, you also will live. On that day you will know that I am in my Father, and you in me, and I in you.' It is a bit like the nesting dolls that we saw on sale in Russia—one contained inside another.

Julian of Norwich was a 14th-century mystic who lived a hermit lifestyle in a cell attached to Norwich Cathedral. She put this truth in her own lyrical way:

We are enfolded in the Father and we are enfolded in the Son and we are enfolded in the Holy Spirit. And the Father is enfolded in us

and the Son is enfolded in us and the Holy Spirit is enfolded in us.
Our soul rests in God, its true peace; our soul stands in God, its
true strength and is deep rooted in God for endless love.[2]

How do we have confidence to join in the dance, though?
Thinking about this, I remembered taking part in a circle-
dancing day. Folk dances from all over the world are
danced in a circle, as an ancient way for people to celebrate
community and togetherness. Our leader began by putting
on a piece of music. She showed us a few simple steps,
which were repeated. She then extended her hand to be
taken by another, who in turn extended her hand to another,
and so on until a chain formed and became a circle. Thus
the dancing began.

Just as Rublev's icon leaves a space for us to enter the circle,
so the Trinity makes space for us to join in. The dance is in
full swing but a hand is extended, as it were, so that we, the
people of God, can join in and live life out of relationship with
the Father, Son and Holy Spirit. This life is to be expressed in
the world in which we live, in our attitudes and actions, our
thoughts and words. God is at work and he calls us to join
him there. When our starting point is God, this will make a
difference to the way we view everything because, all being
well, we will be reflecting, however imperfectly, the way that
God sees the world.

I find that this way of thinking has made a difference in
certain specific areas of my life—in terms of prayer, in my
attitude to God's world, in the ways in which I show care and
in my relationship to the community of the church.

Prayer

Previously, I would have thought of prayer as a conversation with God, which I am expected to initiate. Then, if I have time and I am patient enough, I listen to him. After my prayer, I would wait for an answer—whenever it might come. If no answer was forthcoming, I would blame myself for lack of faith or zeal, as if it depended on me rather than God.

Now I am beginning to realise that to pray is to seek to be where Christ already is—'Christ Jesus, who died, yes, who was raised, who is at the right hand of God, who indeed intercedes for us' (Romans 8:34).

The Holy Spirit is also there to help me when I pray. As Paul writes, again to the Christians in Rome: 'The Spirit helps us in our weakness; for we do not know how to pray as we ought, but that very Spirit intercedes with sighs too deep for words. And God, who searches the heart, knows what is the mind of the Spirit, because the Spirit intercedes for the saints according to the will of God' (8:26–27).

Through his intercessions, Christ makes space for us and creates a meeting place for us and God. The conversation, though, is one that God begins. It is he who speaks to us, inspires us and reveals truth to us. That insight places importance on my attentiveness and receptivity—attentiveness to what God reveals and receptivity of heart to be open to his leading. My part is to respond in whatever way is appropriate and to reflect God's truth in my life.

What if God does not demand prayer so much as he gives prayer? What if prayer simply opens me up to the gift of God's own self? I have always been challenged by the title of a book on prayer by Frank Wallace SJ: *Encounter, Not Performance*.[3]

Prayer is a conversation of love that is already going on in God, for between the persons of the Trinity is everything we mean by prayer—intimacy, adoration, love, self-offering, concern for the world. Our prayer, as God's people, is about joining in that conversation. This is where I find the icon of the Trinity to be a helpful visual aid. It stills my agitation and reminds me that I am in the presence of God the Trinity. Russian mystics describe prayer as 'descending with the mind into the heart' and standing there in the presence of God. Instead of telling God what to do or what I would like to see happen for others, I can simply bring them into the sphere of his divine activity.

For a long time, I had been aware of a longing within me to have some 'hermit' time with God. I dreamed of finding a remote place where I could be alone, but I had no idea if it would ever happen. Eventually, two years ago, while staying in Wales, I 'happened' to hear about a cottage belonging to Ffald-y-Brenin retreat house, which they make available for people on sabbatical or those who need extended thinking time for some reason. As soon as I saw it, I knew, without a shadow of doubt, that this was my place to be.

In the summer, with the blessing of my dear husband, I travelled by train to Fishguard, where I was met, taken to a supermarket to buy food for a fortnight and then delivered to the cottage. Ten miles from Fishguard, off a quiet country road, a rough track led down to the stone cottage, hidden in the fold of a hill. I was without a car, a radio, a television, a phone—all the usual props in life. I also took off my watch so that I would not be governed by time. I had brought with me only a Bible and three books. I did not want to structure my days in such a way that God did not get a look in. To begin with, I felt a little apprehensive. Would I be lonely? Would I be frightened? Would God make himself known to me?

I can truthfully say that I was never lonely. The cottage wrapped itself around me and, when it was fine weather, I sat outside with birds and butterflies for company. Neither was I frightened. I felt safe in that space, even though I could not find a key to fit the locks.

It took me a while to settle into the silence, to become still and at peace, at home to myself and at home with God. Reading Ann Lewin's poem 'Retreat' helped me to let go.

Time out of time,
Resting...
Drifting on Spirit's breath.[4]

I experienced no great revelations or flurry of creativity. It all felt very natural and low-key, but I was aware of the gentle, holding love of God. I realised that if God wanted to love someone like me—who rushes hither and thither, produces this and that and is not certain, at times, that he really loves her—he would surely let her know by quietening her down and then lovingly inhabiting the space in her heart. And that is what happened. Instead of a lot of soul-searching on my part, God simply quietened me with his love. I visited a place within myself that I don't think I had ever really visited before, and I was happy to be there. I left the cottage with a deep sense of belonging to God and belonging to myself.

God's world

On another occasion, I was staying at a convent for an eight-day retreat. It was a beautiful day in late spring and the garden was coming into bloom. The birds were busy feeding their young and bees were on the wing, searching for pollen. From my open window on the second floor, I watched a Sister walking very slowly along a path below me. She kept stopping to smell a blossom, to bend down and look closely at primroses at her feet or to watch a bird as it hopped from branch to branch in the tree above her. As I watched, I felt great pleasure at witnessing her appreciation. After a few minutes a thought struck me: if I had *made* all this natural beauty, how much greater would my pleasure be! It occurred to me that God must experience pleasure when we appreciate what he has created. We come alongside him who 'saw everything that he had made, and indeed, it was very good' (Genesis 1:31).

A friend and I recently put together a programme that includes both quiet days and nature days, to which we have given the title 'Eyes to See'. We recognise that, as Gerard Manley Hopkins wrote, 'The world is charged with the grandeur of God'.[5] Sadly, in the rush of life today, it is so easy to miss that grandeur as we hurry from one place to another.

In our quiet days, we encourage each other to use 'the eyes of our hearts' to gain insight as we spend time alone with God. In our nature days, with our physical eyes we look more closely at the natural world as it changes through the seasons of the year.

This means that we will look for wild orchids or butterflies and moths, find fungi in the autumn woods, and watch starlings at dusk as thousands of them gather to give a stunning aerial display before roosting for the night. We walk through bluebell woods in the spring, chalk meadows in the summer and flaming beech woods in the autumn; we take boats out on the river or go bird-watching.

Sadly, it is all too possible to walk about blind to the glory that is around us, and to miss the unexpected ways that God can come to us. Elizabeth Barrett Browning wrote:

Earth's crammed with heaven,
And every common bush afire with God;
But only he who sees takes off his shoes;
The rest sit round and pluck blackberries.[6]

Evelyn Underhill, in her poem 'Immanence', writes of how the Lord comes to us in little things, if we have eyes to see. Her last verse reads thus:

I come in the little things,
Saith the Lord:
My starry wings
I do forsake,
Love's highway of humility to take:
Meekly I fit My stature to your need.
In beggar's part
About your gates I shall not cease to plead—
Till by such art
I shall achieve My Immemorial Plan.
Pass the low lintel of the human heart.[7]

That is the grace of God: he does not give up on us but finds ways to get through to us, with our limited vision. I find that God often communicates his involvement in my life in small ways that mean something to me but would not mean much to others. He has a way of being specific and very relevant, if we are looking out for him.

I have also drawn inspiration from a reflection by Thomas Merton, written when he was living as a hermit monk in the grounds of a Trappist Monastery in Kentucky, USA:

A spring morning alone in the woods. Sunrise: the enormous yolk of energy spreading and spreading as if to take over the entire sky. After that, the ceremonies of the birds feeding in the wet grass. The meadowlark feeding and singing and then the quiet, totally silent, dry, sun-drenched midmorning of spring, under the climbing sun.

How absolutely central is the truth that we are first of all part of nature, though we are a very special part of nature. We are that part which is conscious of God.[8]

Merton becomes aware that he is surrounded by a natural world—plants, animals, birds and so on—that perfectly obeys the laws of God. There is, however, a gap left open for us—the God-conscious ones, those who are aware of the glory that surrounds us—and that gap allows us to offer it all to God in praise and joy and thanks.

For Merton, being alone under the sky, everything fell into place and he could find his own position in God's created order.

Of course we can see images of God's glory in urban settings, too, if we will look beyond the buildings, the office blocks and the shop windows. I remember one evening when I happened to be in Bristol. The sun was beginning to set and, near the horizon, the sky was coloured orange, red, gold and purple. By chance I looked up, and high in the sky above me I saw a flock of seagulls wheeling in lazy circles, the underside of each bird caught by the colour of the sunset. Against the grey sky of the higher reaches, flaming shapes made an interweaving pattern—*perichoresis* in the sky. It was a wonderful moment, which left me with an overwhelming desire to praise God, to stand in the 'gap' left by nature as Merton described.

Called to care

We are called to join with the Trinity in a desire to care for the earth and see its resources shared fairly among its peoples. In the prayer that Jesus taught his disciples, he prayed: 'Your will be done, on earth as it is in heaven' (Matthew 6:10). The human race is responsible for so much that has damaged our planet-home, not just in environmental terms but for people as well. As God's children, we are called to challenge unjust political, economic and social structures. We are called to press for sustainable methods of food and fuel production, for clean water to be available for everyone. Sometimes I feel overwhelmed by the needs of the world, but I can choose to live responsibly in it and be as generous as possible in supporting agencies that work to alleviate the problems.

Jesus was very closely connected to the world he came to inhabit. This is evident in the Gospel accounts, and especially in his parables. We can be confident that he would call us to move away from overindulgence and exploitation and, instead, to develop attitudes of stewardship and reverence. His desire is that we live in such a way as to bring heaven to earth. He asks us to live from the Trinity, outwards. This is not easy, I find: I have to let myself be reprogrammed time and time again until gradually, little by little, I become more like God the Father, through God the Son, in the power of God the Holy Spirit. The process will take longer than a lifetime but God is infinitely patient and he allows me to be a 'work in progress'.

As we begin to live in closer relationship with God, his values will become ours, and those values will inform our actions. As Paul wrote, 'Do not be conformed to this world, but be transformed by the renewing of your minds, so that you may discern what is the will of God—what is good and acceptable and perfect' (Romans 12:2).

Throughout scripture, we are told clearly that God has a loving bias towards the poor, the broken-hearted and the oppressed. One of David's psalms tells us, for example, 'The Lord is near to the broken-hearted and saves the crushed in spirit' (Psalm 34:18).

The mandate that Jesus took for his own ministry comes from Isaiah 61:1–2. He applied the verses to himself when he spoke in the synagogue of his home town, Nazareth:

The scroll of the prophet Isaiah was given to him. He unrolled the scroll and found the place where it was written: 'The Spirit of the Lord is upon me, because he has anointed me to bring good news to the poor. He has sent me to proclaim release to the captives and recovery of sight to the blind, to let the oppressed go free, to proclaim the year of the Lord's favour.' ... Then he began to say to them, 'Today this scripture has been fulfilled in your hearing.'
(Luke 4:17–19, 21)

Jesus moved freely among those who came to him in need, bringing release, healing and hope.

The dance of the Trinity, which we are invited to join, is not only one of exuberant joy, however. It can also be a dance of lament. We are asked to stand in solidarity with those who suffer, to be a voice for the voiceless and to wait patiently alongside those who need encouraging, helping to bring release from whatever oppresses them. We need, sensitively, to share God's good news of salvation with others. In short, our task is to reflect the heart of God. If we are made in the image of God, we are made in the image of the Trinity, whose life must be expressed in some way in the pattern of our human living.

This, again, is a challenge to the choices I make in life. I may be called to active involvement in some way, which offers help where it is most required and may involve personal cost. This will lead me to look for the right context in which I can play my part. I can also prayerfully and financially support those who bring aid to others, in this country and overseas.

The community of the church

Of course, the *perichoretic* life is limited for us. Although the Holy Spirit can indwell us, we cannot indwell the Holy Spirit in the same way that the Father and the Son indwell him in divine *perichoresis*; nor can we indwell another human being. The same Spirit of God can live in us all, but we cannot live within one another. We are independent human beings, but in our relationships with others we can reflect the mutual cooperation, the love, the giving and receiving that exist in the Trinity, all of which are seen in Rublev's icon.

It would be wonderful if this were a true description of our churches. Instead of power struggles, divisions or obstinacy over style and tradition, we would see a genuine honouring of each other, the people of God in whom the same Spirit dwells.

We would serve one another without feeling threatened. This attitude would release us to be the people God created us to be, both individually and as a community of believers. We would recognise the differing gifts that lie in one another and find contexts in which they could be expressed. Instead of hierarchy, we would create a fellowship built on relationships emanating from God's own love.

We are human beings, though, and this means that we often mess it up and get things wrong. Thank heaven (literally) for the infinite mercy of our God! Just hours before his arrest and subsequent crucifixion, Jesus, knowing our limitations, still prayed:

I ask not only on behalf of these, but also on behalf of those who will believe in me through their word, that they may all be one. As you, Father, are in me and I am in you, may they also be in us, so that the world may believe that you have sent me. The glory that you have given me I have given them, so that they may be one, as we are one, I in them and you in me, that they may become completely one, so that the world may know that you have sent me and have loved them even as you have loved me. (John 17:20–23)

What a privilege and what a high calling—and what an impact such unity would make on the world around!

My husband Paul and I remember a time in the 1970s when we were greatly impacted by the strong sense of unity and life-sharing shown by a group from the United States, who called themselves the Community of Celebration. They came from Houston, Texas, to live in the UK, first in Coventry and then at Yeldall Manor, near Wargrave in Berkshire. We first met them at Ashburnham Place, Sussex, where we had taken our church youth group to join with other young people for a week's house-party. As a community they overflowed with vitality and deep commitment to one another, and visibly demonstrated what it means to be 'the body of Christ'. As often happens when the Holy Spirit is given freedom to be expressed, creativity through music, dance, poetry, art and drama poured out of them. Their singing/worship group was known as The Fisherfolk and they gave many new songs to the church at large. The unity between the members of the community was immediately attractive and their way of being 'real' enabled others to be the same.

As a result of their witness and ministry, a seed took root in our hearts and a longing was born to share our lives with others in some way. After various twists and turns, in 1976 a way opened up for us to buy a property that allowed us to live as an extended family, which we did for several years. Paul and I, our four children and all those who came to share our home look back on that experience as a very formative and influential time in our lives. Of course, there were challenges and issues to work through, but there was also strength in working, praying, eating and playing together that changed all of us and taught us a lot about learning to live in unity.

– For reflection –

What areas of life can you think of that would be radically affected by living out of the heart of God?

Could it make a difference to a difficult relationship or a situation at work?

How would it affect your attitude towards someone you find hard to love?

Would it change your reaction to criticism or seeming rejection?
How about times when you feel fearful or anxious?

Jeu d'esprit

Flame-dancing Spirit, come
Sweep us off our feet and
Dance us through our days.
Surprise us with your rhythms,
Dare us to try new steps, explore
New patterns and new partnerships.
Release us from old routines,
To swing in abandoned joy
And fearful adventure.
And in the intervals,
Rest us,
In your still centre.
ANN LEWIN[9]

— Chapter 8 —

Now and for ever

We live in a noisy, fast-moving world where we are bombarded by images, sounds and words, both spoken and written. So many things come to us at the press of a button—TV and radio programmes, music, food cooked in a microwave, an image recorded on a camera, communication with others across the globe via the internet and telephone, and access to vast quantities of information stored on the worldwide web. It is a beautiful world but a world also of turmoil, anxiety and extremes. With so much to concern and distract us, it is not easy to take time to absorb spiritual realities. It feels like swimming against the current, the fast flow of today's society, and it takes an act of discipline to stop and consider just what God the Trinity offers us—which is nothing less than eternal life. As William Barclay writes, 'Eternal life is the life of God and to have eternal life is to share in the life of God.'[1]

When we respond in faith to God's offer of salvation through Christ and to his calling on our lives, we receive this gift of eternal life, a quality of life that begins now and continues in heaven. We live in the kingdom of this world but at the same time we live in the kingdom of heaven. If you can imagine two circles alongside each other but overlapping slightly, we live, as it were, in the overlap. We experience something of the life of God now but not fully, not as we will in heaven. At present we live in two realms and inevitably there are tensions, as summarised in the words of American historian and theologian Rufus M. Jones: 'The real business of life... is to piece this life with the life of heaven, to see it as one with all eternity, a part of it, a life within it.'[2]

We are called to bring heaven to earth in our attitudes and actions. This is why Jesus taught us to pray, 'Our Father in heaven, hallowed be your name. Your kingdom come. Your will be done, on earth as it is in heaven' (Matthew 6:9–10).

God asks us to live fully in this present world, but at the same time we need to have our sights set on the realm of God, as David Adam writes:

We need to keep a vision of this other world. Not as a place far away or set in another time, but a world that keeps breaking into our lives. Not a world that runs parallel to ours, but a world that is closely interwoven with ours, in fact a world in which our world shares and into which we can enter.[3]

Through scripture, through worship, through the arts (including icons such as Rublev's), through music, nature and so on, we are opened up to the life of God and the kingdom of heaven. Sometimes we have experiences which make us sense that 'the veil is thin between heaven and earth'—an expression from the spirituality of the Celtic church. There are certain places that can be described as 'thin' places, where the realms of heaven and earth seem especially close together. These are usually places where prayer has been offered over many centuries. For me and, I think, for many others, the islands of Iona and Lindisfarne possess that special quality, and pilgrims journey there from across the world to experience it.

I remember a similar experience in 1972, when the Christian Festival of Light took place in London. There was a march and a rally in Trafalgar Square in the afternoon, and in the evening around 20,000 people gathered in Hyde Park for further addresses and singing. There was a point at which gentle rain began to fall and the vast crowd started to sing, unaccompanied, the Lord's Prayer. As the swell of voices rose to sing the words, 'For thine is the kingdom, the power and the glory', I thought the heavens would open and we would see Christ in glory. It was a powerful moment, when the veil seemed very thin.

Heaven is closer than we realise. In life we get glimpses of glory but, for the most part, we live in the mist that calls for faith. Yet there will come a day when all will be revealed and we shall see our God clearly, in all his glory. As Paul writes to the church in Corinth: 'Now we see in a mirror, dimly [mirrors in New Testament times were made of polished brass], but then we will see face to face. Now I know only in part; then I will know fully, even as I have been fully known' (1 Corinthians 13:12).

Evangeline Paterson picks up this thought in her poem, 'And that will be heaven':

and that will be heaven

and that will be heaven
at last   the first unclouded
seeing

*   to stand like the sunflower*
turned full face to the sun   drenched
with light   in the still centre
held   while the circling planets
hum with an utter joy

> *seeing and knowing*
> *at last   in every particle*
> *seen and known   and not turning*
> *away*
>
> *never turning away*
> *again.*[4]

I like the idea of seeing and not needing to turn away—perhaps with a sense of unworthiness—but standing full-faced towards our God, knowing him and being fully known by him. That is freedom unlimited. Borrowing the title from my first chapter, it will indeed be 'the long look'.

Our physical senses are a means to an end. There will come a day when spiritual realities will no longer need to be communicated through words, icons, sacraments and symbols. Having led us by many paths into the presence of God, our senses will recede into the background of praise and prayer. Their work will be done.

Until that day, we can live gratefully for the work of the Trinity in our lives—for the love of the Father, for the grace of Jesus Christ and for the fellowship of the Holy Spirit. We can look forward to seeing the Trinity face to face and to the wonderful reunions that will take place in heaven. To God be the glory!

~ For reflection ~

I suggest that you read the following passages from Revelation and let God lead you in your imagination to visualise something of the splendours of heaven. We find in these passages a blend of glory and majesty with intimacy and gentleness.

Revelation 4:1–8
Revelation 21:1–5

Rublev's icon centres on the sacrificial cup, which is being blessed by God the Father, God the Son (who is the Lamb of God) and God the Holy Spirit. In Revelation we read of the glory given to 'the Lamb that was slaughtered'—Jesus, who is now seated at the right hand of God in majesty.

'Worthy is the Lamb that was slaughtered
to receive power and wealth and wisdom and might
and honour and glory and blessing!'
Then I heard every creature in heaven and on earth and under the
earth and in the sea, and all that is in them, singing,
'To the one seated on the throne and to the Lamb
be blessing and honour and glory and might
forever and ever. (Revelation 5:11–13)

If you have a recording of Handel's Messiah, you may like to play the track that begins 'Worthy is the Lamb'.

~ Prayers ~

O God, you are the one to whom I reach out,
mystery beyond human thinking, love beyond our comprehending.
Yet because you are love, you have reached out to me,
joined me to Christ,
Taken me into the very heart of your divine life,
Come close to me as father and brother.
And even more. You yourself have come to dwell in me,
so it is your love within me reaching out to your love beyond me.
O God beyond me, God beside me, God within me![5]

O God our mystery,
you bring us to life,
call us to freedom,
and move between us with love.
May we so participate
in the dance of your Trinity,
that our lives may resonate with you,
now and forever. Amen.[6]

— Notes —

Chapter 1

1 Sister Wendy Beckett, *The Gaze of Love* (Marshall Pickering, 1993).

Chapter 2

1 Eusebius, *The History of the Church*, chapter 7, section 18.
2 V. Lossky and L.Ouspensky, *The Meaning of Icons* (SVS Press, revd edn 1982), p. 43.
3 Gillian Allnutt, 'Preparing the Icon' from *How the Bicycle Shone: New & Selected Poems* (Bloodaxe Books, 2007).
4 Jim Forest, *Praying with Icons* (Orbis Books, revd edn 2008), p. 31.
5 Ann Lewin, *Watching for the Kingfisher* (Canterbury Press, 2009), p. 16.

Chapter 3

1 M. Klimenko, *The 'Vita' of St Sergii of Radonezh* (Nordland Publishing, 1980), p. 182.

Chapter 4

1 See Gabriel Bunge, *The Rublev Trinity* (SVS Press, 2007), pp. 24–41, for more on interpretations of the scene.
2 Lossky and Ouspensky, *Meaning of Icons*, p. 204.

Chapter 5

1 Irenaeus, *The Lion Christian Quotation Collection* (Lion, 1997), p. 13.
2 Henri Nouwen, *Behold the Beauty of the Lord* (Ave Maria Press, 1987), pp. 20, 21.
3 George Herbert, *The Complete English Poems* (Penguin Classics, 1991), p. 178.

Chapter 6

1 Alister McGrath, *The Christian Vision of God* (SPCK, 2008), pp. 74, 75.
2 T.S. Eliot, 'Burnt Norton' from *Four Quartets* (Faber and Faber, 1944), p. 5.

Chapter 7

1 Sydney Carter, 'Lord of the Dance' (Stainer Bell).
2 Julian of Norwich, *Enfolded in Love* (DLT, 1980), p. 34.
3 Frank Wallace SJ, *Encounter, Not Performance* (E.J. Dwyer, 1991).
4 Lewin, *Watching for the Kingfisher*, p. 16.
5 Gerard Manley Hopkins, *Poems and Prose* (Penguin Classics, 1953), p. 27.
6 Elizabeth Barrett Browning, from *Aurora Leigh* (Oxford World's Classics, 2008).
7 Evelyn Underhill, *An Anthology of the Love of God* (Mowbray, 1953), p. 54.
8 Thomas Merton, *The Shining Wilderness* (DLT, 1988), p. 17.
9 Lewin, *Watching for the Kingfisher*, p. 89.

Chapter 8

1 William Barclay, *The Gospel of John Vol. 1*, (Saint Andrew Press, 1965), p. 129.
2 Rufus M. Jones, *Spiritual Reformers in the 16th and 17th Centuries* (Macmillan, 1914), p. 335.
3 David Adam, *Borderlands* (SPCK, 1991), p. 211.
4 Evangeline Paterson, from ed. Mary Batchelor, *The Lion Christian Poetry Collection* (Lion, 1995), p. 494.
5 Richard Harries, from ed. Angela Ashwin, *The Book of a Thousand Prayers* (Marshall Pickering, 1996), p. 342.
6 Janet Morley, *All Desires Known* (SPCK, 1992), p. 18.

The Jesus Prayer

Simon Barrington-Ward

The Jesus Prayer has been known and loved by generations of Christians. Originating in the Orthodox Church, it is a way of entering into the river of prayer that flows from the heart of God, as Jesus continually prays for his people and for the world he loves. Within us, too, the Spirit of God prays 'with sighs too deep for words', and the Jesus Prayer can help us to join in the loving intercession of God-in-Christ for the redemption of all things.

In this new edition of a BRF classic, Simon Barrington-Ward teaches us how to use the prayer, and provides biblical and historical background for understanding its significance.

ISBN 978 1 84101 588 0   £5.99
Available from your local Christian bookshop or, in case of difficulty, direct from BRF using the order form opposite.

About
brf:

BRF is a registered charity and also a limited company, and has been in existence since 1922. Through all that we do—producing resources, providing training, working face-to-face with adults and children, and via the web—we work to resource individuals and church communities in their Christian discipleship through the Bible, prayer and worship.

Our Barnabas children's team works with primary schools and churches to help children under 11, and the adults who work with them, to explore Christianity creatively and to bring the Bible alive.

To find out more about BRF and its core activities and ministries, visit:

www.brf.org.uk
www.brfonline.org.uk
www.barnabasinschools.org.uk
www.barnabasinchurches.org.uk
www.messychurch.org.uk
www.foundations21.org.uk

If you have any questions about BRF and our work, please email us at

enquiries@brf.org.uk

ORDERFORM

REF	TITLE	PRICE	QTY	TOTAL
588 0	The Jesus Prayer	£5.99		

POSTAGE AND PACKING CHARGES						
Order value	UK	Europe	Surface	Air Mail	Postage and packing	
£7.00 & under	£1.25	£3.00	£3.50	£5.50	Donation	
£7.10–£30.00	£2.25	£5.50	£6.50	£10.00	**TOTAL**	
Over £30.00	FREE	prices on request				

Name _____ Account Number _____

Address _____

_____ Postcode _____

Telephone Number_____

Email _____

Payment by: ❏ Cheque ❏ Mastercard ❏ Visa ❏ Postal Order ❏ Maestro

Card no ❏❏❏❏ ❏❏❏❏ ❏❏❏❏ ❏❏❏❏ ❏❏❏

Valid from ❏❏❏❏ Expires ❏❏❏❏ Issue no. ❏❏❏

Security code* ❏❏❏ *Last 3 digits on the reverse of the card.
ESSENTIAL IN ORDER TO PROCESS YOUR ORDER   Shaded boxes for Maestro use only

Signature _____ Date _____

All orders must be accompanied by the appropriate payment.

Please send your completed order form to:
BRF, 15 The Chambers, Vineyard, Abingdon OX14 3FE
Tel. 01865 319700 / Fax. 01865 319701 Email: enquiries@brf.org.uk

❏ Please send me further information about BRF publications.

Available from your local Christian bookshop.   BRF is a Registered Charity

95